A Short Introduction To Swedish Grammar : Adapted For The Use Of Englishmen

Brunnmark, Gustavus

A SHORT

Introduction

TO

SWEDISH GRAMMAR,

ADAPTED

FOR

THE USE OF ENGLISHMEN.

BY

GUSTAVUS BRUNNMARK, M. A.

CHAPLAIN TO THE SWEDISH LEGATION AT THE COURT OF GREAT
BRITAIN, &c.

The Second edition.

STOCKHOLM:

Printed by Charles Deleen.

1826.

HAVING frequently been invited to instruct English Gentlemen in the Swedish Language, my endeavors to be of essential use to them, and with as little loss of time as possible, experienced considerable impediments through want of a suitable Swedish and English Grammar, this, together with the request of several of my most esteemed scholars, has induced me to submit to the Public the annexed Introduction to a Swedish and English Grammar.

Respecting the arrangement of this work, I shall at present make no apology; it must speak for itself. It is merely a sketch, intended for beginners, who, having hitherto had no short and methodical plan to assist their memory, will not expect any thing like perfection in a first attempt, and even, I hope, readily excuse, that the pen of a foreigner frequently betrays itself.

The mistakes I may labour under in the Swedish will in due time by detected, and when corrected and cleared of every thing objectionable, I trust to have the honor of submitting my GRAMMAR to the Public, to which work I mean the present as an introduction, and object for critical improvement only.

In spelling the language I have followed the rules laid down by the Swedish Academy, in their excellent Treatise on that subject; the perusal of which I earnestly recommend to my scholars. In the Grammatical Institutes, as I have had no complete pattern to go by, but often been obliged to walk in an unbeaten track, I have stated with due deference what has appeared to me to be the most correct, and will gladly embrace the first opportunity to correct what may be wrong in my present statements.

I take this opportunity of acknowledging the favor conferred on me by my Subscribers, among whom I find many of those respectable characters to whom I have had the honor of giving lessons in the Swedish Language.

A SHORT

Introduction

TO

SWEDISH GRAMMAR.

Of the ALPHABET *and the* SOUNDS *of the Letters.*

The Swedish Alphabet consists of twenty-eight Letters, of wich nine are

> VOWELS, viz.

A sounds like the English *a* in *psalm, psalm.*

E has a sound between the *slender a* and the *e,* or as it is commonly pronounced in the article *the, de.*

I sounds like the English *ee* in *bee, bi.*

O (the Greek *ω*) sounds nearest to the *narrow oo* in *rood.*

U Sounds like the English *u* in *ruin, ruin.*

Y — — the French *u* in *une, syn,* sight.

Å — — the English *o* in *long, lång.*

Ä — — the English *a* in *name, nämna.*

Ö — — the French *eu* in *feu; bröd,* bread, or nearest to *i* before *r,* as in *thirsty, törstig.*

And nineteen CONSONANTS.

B	say	be	N	say	n
C		ce	P		pe
D		de	Q		ku
F		f	R		err
G		ge	S		s
H		hå	T		te
J		långt i (i. e. *long i*)	V		ve
K		kå	X		ex
L		l	Z		sätah
M		m			

Obs. The Swedish pronunciation of b, c, d, g, p, t, and v, differs from the English in the same degree as the sound of the letter *e* differs in the two languages.

All the vowels retain constantly their genuine sound as above, except *e* and *o*, of which the former sometimes takes that of *ä*, the latter that of *å* 1), as *den*, *folk*, read dänn, fålk.

Every vowel, even *e* final, must be distinctly pronounced, as *pelare* pillar, not *pelar*.

The Swedish language has no diphthongs.

---

1) Commonly when consonants of a double sound follow, see note 4, page 9 a) b). I deem it superfluous to say more on this head, as the genuine sounds of *e*, and particularly of *o*, in the Swed. lang. cannot be ascertained by signs, but must be learnt by hearing. Those, who may wish to see this subject fully discussed, will find it in *Svenska Akademiens Handlingar*. The transactions of the Swedish Academy, Stockholm, 1801. Vol. I. page 103, and following.

When two vowels occur together, they must both be heard, as *bēēdiga*, *bröär*.

Of the vowels four are *hard*, viz. *a, o, u, å;* the other five, *e, i, y, ä, ö, soft*. I call them so by way of distinction, because some consonants (c, ch, g, k, and sk) before the former have a harder sound, before the latter a softer. NB. When they belong to the same syllable.

C before the hard, sounds as *k*, before the soft as *s: Cato, Citron*, read Kato, Sitron.

CH occur only in foreign words and proper names, and are pronounced before the hard vowels (and at the end of words) as k, before the soft as tj: *Charon, China*, read Karon, Tjina (Cawron, Cheenah).

G before the hard, sounds as *g* in *good*, before the soft as the Swed. j, (or Eng. y): *ge* 2), *gille, gynna, gäst, göra*, read je, jille, jynna, jäst, jöra.

K before the hard, sounds as *k* in *king;* before the soft as tj: *ked, kid, kyss, kär, köp*, read tjed, tjid, tjyss, tjär, tjöp.

Sk before the hard, sounds as *sk* in *skull*, before the soft as the Swed. sj, (or Eng. sh); *sked*,

---

2) If *e* (or *i*) belongs to a nominal or verbal termination (as in *mogen, dragen*, or to the definite article (se page 15) added to a noun ending with *g*, (as in *sången, lagen*), then *g* retains its primitive sound. The same observation relates also to the other above mentioned changeable consonants. The nominal terminations here alluded to are chiefly *e, el, en, er, eri, ig, isk, &c.*

skida, sky, skär, skön, read sjed, sjida, sjy, sjär, sjön.

---

f in the end of a word is always pronounced as v 3), *af, bref*, read av, brev; and if the word be augmented, a *v* is put in after *f*, as *graf*, (grave) plural *grafvar*, and *f* loses its sound, which it always does before *v*, except the word be compounded, as *afvända*, to avert; *brefväska*, letterbag; read then avvända, brevväska.

g at the end of a syllable, when preceded by another consonant (except *n*), is generally heard as j: *talg*, tallow; *vargskinn*, wolfskin, read talj, varjskinn.

When *gn* end a syllable, they are heard nearly as *ngn: regn*, rain, *vagn*, coach; read rengn, vangn.

h before *j* and *v* loses its aspiration: *hjelp, hvilken*, read jelp, vilken.

k before *n* as also *v* or *w* (if it be used) before *r*, are both distinctly heard, as in *knä*, knee; *vrång*, wrong.

stj sounds like the Sw. *sj* (or Eng. sh) as *stjerna*, star, read sjerna (shernah).

th and *w* have both lost their original sound

3) The same may be said when it is the last letter of any syllable, if we only attend to the original spelling of the same. *Afton, efter, ofta*, &c. are no exceptions, for *f* is here (though commonly spelt so) not the last letter in the syllable: it therefore retains its genuine sound; but in *brefbok, skriftyg*, &c. the case is different: being here originally the last, we of course read brevbok, skrivtyg.

in the Swedish language. If *th* occurs, it is heard as *t*, and *w* as *v*.

Consonants must not be pronounced as double, unless written so 4): *hat*, hatred; *vis*, wise, read *hawt*, *vees;* but when doubled, they should always be heard so as *hatt*, hat; *viss*, certain; *all*, all; particularly as many words, of a very different signification, are only hereby distinguished from each other, as *hat* and *hatt; ful*, foul; *full*, full; *hop*, heap; *hopp*, hope, &c.

Of the Noun Substantive.

The noun substantive is either Masculine, Feminine, or Neuter 5), and is inflected after five

4) Except (a) such consonants as have a double sound in themselves, as *j*, *x*, and for the most part *m*, as *ej*, not; *vax; kom*, come, read *kämm*.

(b) When two consonants end a syllable, the former commonly sounds double, as *stark*, strong; *verk*, work, read starrk, *värrk;* but it requires some knowledge of the language before it is possible to tell which, or how many letters originally belong to a syllable, ex. gr. *n* in *benknota*, knuckle, is not doubled, because we spell *ben-knota;* but in *bänkrad*, row of benches, it is, because *n* and *k* here belong to the same syllable, as bänk-rad.

(c) The last consonant in a short syllable, as *n* and *d* in *gifven*, *hatad*.

(d) The letter *n*, when the last in short monosyllables, is doubled, as in *han, hon* (she) *den, din, in, man, men, min, sin;* but their number is but small.

5) The different genders have no fixed characteristics. It seems however as if the declensions nearest decided them: thus all nouns of the *first* are feminine, all of the *fourth* and *fifth* neuter; but to tell whether nouns of the second and third declensions are masculine or feminine, is not so easy. I would here, as the same article *(en)* is applied to both (see the head articles, page 15) follow the

declensions, which are distinguished by their terminations in plural, viz.

The 1st ends in plural in or: *böna*, bean; pl. *bönor*.

The 2d — — — in ar: *ring*, ring; pl. *ringar*.

The 3d — — — in er: *park*, park; pl. *parker*.

The 4th adds in plural an n: *fäste*, hold; pl. *fästen*.

The 5th is the same in sing. and pl. *band*, band;
pl. *band*.

The *cases* are expressed by the context or by
particles. One only is inflected, viz. the genitive,
which is formed by adding an *s* to the nominative,
as *ring*, gen. *rings*. The particles thus used are
af, of; *åt*, *til*, to; *o!* O; *från*, from.

Some nouns are only used in singular, as *hopp*,
talg, *hjelp*; and almost all ending with *an*, as
längtan, longing; others only in plural, as *föräld-
rar*, parents; *syskon*, brothers and sisters; *kläder*, clothes; and some have an irregular plural,
as *lus* louse, pl. *löss*; *gås*, goose, pl. *gäss*; *öga*,
eye, pl. *ögon*; *öra*, ear, pl. *öron*, &c.

example of the Danish Grammarians, and above all, that of Profes-
sor Jac. Baden, in his *Forelæsninger over det Danske Sprog,*
Lectures on the Danish Language, and with him admit of a common gender, if what he says C. iv. p. 58. of the introduction of
den (that or it) for *han* and *hun* (he and she) was equally appli-
cable to the Swedish. In many instances it is so; but as I am un-
willing to proceed upon uncertainties, I will await the decision of
the Sw. Academy, and, suppressing my own rules and exceptions,
at present recommend practice as the only means of attaining a
just knowledge in this matter.

First Declension, plural in or.

Nouns of the first declension end with an *a* in singular, which is left out in plural, and are all feminine, as

Sing. nom. *Penna*, pen; Plur. n. *pennor.*
    gen. *pennas,*   g. *pennors.*

Second Declension, plural in ar.

Nouns of different terminations in singular belong to this declension, and are either masculine or feminine, as

S. n. *Penning,* coin, pl. *penningar,* M. *Själ,* soul, pl. *själar* F.
  g. *pennings*   *penningars.* g *själs*   *själars.*

Obs. a. Nouns of this declension, ending with *e* in singular, leave out that *e* in plural, as *påle,* pole; *fåle,* fole; pl. *pålar, fålar;* but all other vowels remain.

b. The plural termination *ar,* suffers no contraction, although the noun end with a vowel, as *sky,* sky, pl. *skyar; å,* river, pl. *åar; ö,* island, pl. *öar.*

c. In the singular number, if the letter, preceding the last in a word of this declension, be a vowel, then that vowel is left out in plural, as *himmel,* heaven; *afton,* evening; *syster, sommar;* pl. *himlar, aftnar, systrar, somrar.* But if the word be monosyllabic, the vowel must be retained, as *sten,* stone; *dal,* dale, pl. *stenar, dalar.*

d. In a few nouns, belonging to this declension, the *o* in singular is changed into *ö* in plural, as *moder*, mother; *dotter*, daughter; pl. *mödrar*, *döttrar*.

Third Declension, plural in er.

Nouns of this declension are also variously terminated in singular, and are (with one exception only) masculine or feminine, as

S. n. *Planet*, pl. *planeter*, M. s. n. *Mark*, land, pl. *marker*, F.
g. *planets*, *planeters*.   g. *marks*,   *markers*.

If a noun of this declension end in singular with a vowel, *r* only is added in plural, as *hustru*, wife; *sko*, shoe; *tå*, toe; plur. *hustrur, skor, tår*, instead of *hustruer*, &c. *Obs.* Nouns of the neuter gender, (all of which end with i) are excepted from this rule, as *bryggeri*, brewery; *fiskeri;* pl. *bryggerier, fiskerier.* Also words adopted from foreign languages of whatever gender they may be, provided they belong to this declension; as *akademi, armé, idé, fé, staty,* pl. *akademier, arméer,* &c.

In some words of this declension also, the vowel in singular is changed into another in plural, as *hand*, pl. *händer; fot,* pl. *fötter; tång*, pl. *tänger*, tongs.

Fourth Declension.

Nouns of this declension are all neuter, and terminate in singular with a vowel, to which an *n* is added in plural, as *hjerta*, heart; pl. *hjertan: knä*, knee, pl. *knän; bo*, nest, pl. *bon; kläde*, cloth, pl. *kläden;* *bi,* bee; pl. *bin;* and are inflected as all others in the genitive case.

Fifth Declension.

Nouns of this declension, or such as are the same in singular and plural, are neuter, and of different terminations, as *segel,* sail and sails; *rum,* room and rooms. Except only those ending with *are,* which are all masc. as, *bagare,* baker and bakers, &c.

Of the ADJECTIVES.

An adjective has generally three degrees of comparison, viz. the Positive, the Comparative, and the Superlative. The termination *are,* added to the positive, makes the regular comparative, and *ast* the superlative; as *glad, gladare, gladast.* NB. A few leave out the *a,* retaining only *re* and *st,* as *hög,* high, *högre, högst,* not *högare, högast,* &c.

Such adjectives as do not admit of a regular comparison, express the comp. and superl. degrees by *mer* and *mest,* more, most; or *mindre* and *minst,* less, least. Of this kind are chiefly all ending with *ad* (except *glad*) and such as are formed of proper names, all of which end in *sk,* as *platonisk,* platonic; *Romersk,* Roman; we cannot say *platoniskare, Romerskast,* &c.

Some adjectives have lost their positive degree, which is supplied by another word of the same (or nearest) signification. Such are ex. gr. *värre, värst,* worse, worst (posit. *elak,* bad); *sämre,* inferior, *sämst* (posit. *dålig*, good for nothing, weak) &c.

Adjectives not monosyllabic, ending with *al*, *el*, *en*, and *er*, when these syllables are not accentuated, (which they are in a few adopted words) leave out the *a* and the *e* in the comparisons *), as *gammal*, old; *dubbel*, double; *trogen*, true; *mager*, meagre; comp. *gamlare*, *dubblare*, not *gammalare*, *dubbelare*, &c.

Adjectives are declined in the genitive case, by adding an *s* to the nominative, as *glad*, gen. *glads;* comp. *gladares.* The superlative degree does not admit of an absolute or indefinite genitive case: We cannot say *gladasts*; and if we say *gladastes*, we speak definitely; but of this I will treat in its proper place.

Adjectives ending with *s* admit of an absolute or indefinite genitive case only in the comparative degree, as *visares.* We can as little say *vis's* as *visasts.*

Adjectives have three genders, of which the Masculine and Feminine in singular are always the same, as *glad man, glad moder;* but the Neuter is formed by adding a *t*, as *gladt folk*, unless the word ends with *t* or *en*. In the former ease it is the same through all the genders, as *fast, salt;* in the latter, *en* is changed into *et*, as *liten*, neut. *litet*.

---

*) Also in the plural number and in the definite state, see seqv.

The plural number is formed by adding *e* or *a* to the positive singular, as *glad*, pl. *glade*, or *glada* 6). The comparative and superlative degrees are the same in both numbers, as *vis*, pl. *vise*, or *visa*, comp. *visare*, sup. *visast*.

Adjectives, ending with *a*, are (through all the genders) the same both in singular and plural, as *bra*, good; *ringa*, poor, low; *stilla*, quiet, &c.

Of the ARTICLES.

The articles are two, viz. the Indefinite and the Definite.

The indefinite is *en* (a) for the masculine and feminine gender, and *et* for the neuter, as *en konung*, a king; *en drottning*, a queen; *et ting*, a thing.

The definite state is also expressed by *en* and *et;* but in this case the article is added to the noun, as *konungen*, the king; *drottningen*, the queen; *tinget*, the thing.

If the noun ends with a vowel, then only *n* or *t* is added to make it definite; as *hustru*, wife; *arbete*, work; defin. *hustrun*, *arbetet*, not *hustruen*, *arbeteet*. From this rule are excepted those of the third declension ending with *i*, as *fiskeri;*

---

6) *e* was formerly meant for the masculine gender only, as *a* is still for the feminine and neuter; but in later times *a* is (with a few exceptions) used as well for the masculine as for the other two genders, just as the euphony requires.

def. *fiskeriet*, not *fiskerit;* and nouns of that declension, adopted from foreign languages, as *akademi, té*, tea; def. *akademien, téet*, as also monosyllabic nouns of the fourth declension, ex. gr. *knä, bi;* def. *knäet, biet.*

Such nouns as end with *an* and *en*, and have no plural, do not admit the addition of the definite article, as *tran*, train oil; *fruktan*, fear; *borgen*, bail, &c.

The *e* of definite article is also generally left out, when the word ends with *el* or *er*, and is not monosyllabic, as *mantel, hunger;* def. *manteln, hungern* 7). Except those of the fifth declension, which retain the *e* of the article, both in singular and plural, but throw away the *e* of their own termination, as *hagel*, hail; def. *haglet*, not *hagelt* or *hagelet.*

The article *en*, neut. *et*, has an obsolete plural, *ene* or *ena*, (see note 6) as *små ena*, little ones; and although it is no longer used by itself in writing, it is constantly added to plural nouns to make them definite, when however only the terminations *ne*, or *na* are retained, as *konungarne*, not *konungarene* the kings; *bönorna*, not *bönorena,*

---

7) That the word *himmel*, heaven (and two or three more) when used emphatically, either retain the full construction, as *himmelen*, or leave out the *e* of their own termination, as *himlen*, does not seem of sufficient weight to alter the rule.

norena, the beans. Nouns of the fifth decl. (all but those ending with *are*) are here again an exception; as they leave out the *e* or *a* final of the plural article, retaining only *en* to make them def. in plural, as *hagel, ben;* pl. def. *haglen,* the hailstones; *benen,* the bones, not *hagelna, benna.*

The adjectives have also a Definite termination, namely, *e* or *a*, added to the positive degree, as *glade* or *glada* (see note 6); and an *e* (the comparative has *e* before) to the superlative, as *gladaste*, gen. *gladastes;* thus the positive singular in the *definite state*, is the same as the positive plural, which the context must distinguish, as also whether the adjective stands in singular or plural, which when definite always are alike. For instance, *store konung! store konungar! store konungar finnas.* Here *store* is used three different ways: The first is definite singular, the second definite plural, and the third is a simple plural. But this will be more clearly seen hereafter.

As the article never stands by itself, but must be supported by a noun, 8) so when pronouns (whose characteristic on the contrary it is to stand by themselves, and assume the power of other nouns) do not supply the place of other nouns, but only serve to ascertain one; they seem rather

8) See APOLLONIUS de Syntaxi, L. i. C. 3. L. ii. C. 8.

2

to fall into the species of articles 9). But besides this, every pronoun in the Swedish language is in itself either definite or indefinite, which best appears from the power the have on the adjectives; for all definite pronouns place the following adjectives in the definite state, whilst the indefinite leave the adjectives also indefinite.

The Definite are chiefly the Personal, Possessive, and Demonstrative pronouns, as *Jag*, I; *du*, thou; &c. *min*, my, or mine; *din*, thy, or thine; *den*, that; *denne*, this, &c.

The Indefinite are, *Hvar* and *hvarje*, every; *hvar och en*, every one; *hvem* and *hvilken* 10), *hvad*, what; *ingen*, no or none; *sådan*, such; *en annan*, another; *hvar annan*, every other; *all*, all; *mången*, many, &c.

On substantives the pronouns have very little influence. Such only as can be definitely expressed themselves, place, when so used, the substantives in the definite state. Of this description are ex. gr. the three following: *Sjelf*, self, defin. *sjelfve* or *sjelfva;* *en*, one, def. *ene* or *ena;* *annan*, other, def. *andre* or *andra*, as *sjelfva saken, ena*

---

9) See Varro De Ling. Lat. L. vii.

10) When it signifies *what* or *what a*, as *hvilken stor dag!* what a great day! but when it answers to *which*, the subsequent adjective must always be in the definite state, as *hvilken stora dag skall komma*, which great day is to come.

handen, andra boken. We cannot say, *sjelfva sak, ena hand, andra bok.*

But of all the pronouns there is none partakes so much of the nature of an article as *den,* neutr. *det,* for besides that it always makes the following adjective definite, it also, when used as a pronoun, (signifying that or *that very*) places the substantive 11) in the definite state, as *jag har den boken,* I have that book. But it is often used as a mere demonstrative particle, when it leaves the substantive in the indefinite state, as *den skillnad som är,* the difference which is; and it then answers to *the* in the English.

Observe here also, that *denne,* this, when used more demonstratively (signifying the same as *den här, this very*) always requires the following substantive to be definite: Thus, *denna boken,* means this (very) book; *denna bok* simply, this book.

Of the Pronouns.

The Pronouns have been considered under the preceding head, as far as they appear as articles 12). As nouns they will best be learnt by attending to the opposite English words, as

11) Except proper names, and sometimes words denoting the affections of the mind (when used emphatically) as *hat,* hatred; *kärlek,* love, &c.

12) See further on this subject Harris's Hermes, or Philosophical Inquiry concerning Universal Grammar, B. i. C. 5. B. ii. C. 1.

Singular.		*Plural.*	
Jag,	I.	*Vi,*	we.
Mig,	me.	*Oss,*	us.
Du,	thou.	*J,*	you.
Dig,	thee.		
Sig.	himself, herself, itself, & themselves.		

Singular.

Han,	he.	*Hon,*	she.	*Det,*	it.
Hans,	his.	*Hennes,*	her or hers.	*Dess,*	its.
Honom,	him.	*Henne,*	her.		

Plural.

De,	they.
Deras,	their or theirs.
Dem,	them.

Sing. *Min,* neutr. *mitt,* my or mine.

Din, neutr. *ditt,* thy or tine.

Plur. *Mine* or *mina* (see note 6, p. 15) gen. *minas.*

Dine or *dina;* gen. *dinas.*

Sing. *Vår,* neutr. *vårt,* our or ours.

Eder, neutr. *edert,* your or yours.

Plur. *Våre* or *våra,* gen. *våras.*

Edre or *edra,* gen. *edras.*

Sing. *Sin,* neutr. *sitt,* his, her or hers, and its.

Plur. *Sine* or *sina.* gen. *sinas,* their or theirs.

An example will best prove the use of this pronoun: *Han tog sin hatt,* he took his (own) hat

Han tog hans hatt, he took his (another's) hat.
Pl. *De togo sina* 13) *hattar.*

Singular.	*Singular:*
Nom. *Den,* neutr. *det,* that.	Nom. *Denne* or *denna,* neutr. *detta,* this.
Gen. *Dens.*	Gen. *Dennes* or *dennas,* n. *dettas.*

Plural.	*Plural.*
De, those.	*Desse* or *dessa,* these. Gen. *dessas.*

Singular.

N. *Annan,* other, neutr. *annat.* Gen. *annans, annats.*
Defin. *andre* or *andra.*   Gen. *andras.*

Plural.

Nom. *Andre* or *andra.* Gen. *andras.*

Obs. The definite singular of this pronoun (as well as of *sjelf.*) is the same as the plural, which, if not made definite by *de,* leaves the following substantive in the indefinite state, as *andra hattar,* or *de andra hattarne.* This latter observation however does not relate to *sjelf,* which, when used as an adjective pronoun, always places its substan-

---

13) There are some who never use *sin* and *sina,* when the preceding noun or pronoun to which it refers stands in plural; but always in that case *deras,* as *de togo deras hattar,* they took their hats; *De älska deras (sitt) barn,* they love their child. But though this is correct in the French and German Languages, and strongly commended by Mr. BADEN, in the Danish, (see C. x. p. 90 of his Lectures) I have here only consulted the late publications of the Swed. Academy, and therefore stated the above without regard to the custom of a few, or to the analogy of other languages.

tive in the definite state; we cannot say, *sjelfva hattar*, but *sjelfva hattarne.*

Ho and *hvem*, who, (*hvems*, whose, *hvem*, whom) are used in questions.

Hvilken, neutr. *hvilket;* gen. *hvilkens, hvilkets;* pl. *hvilke* or *hvilka;* gen. *hvilkas.* This pronoun answers to *who, which,* and *what,* and is used both as a simple relative and in questions.

Som, the common subjunctive pronoun, answers to *who, which,* and *that.* It is used both after persons and things, and never begins a sentence.

Hvar, neutr. *hvart,* every, gen. *hvars;* (this genitive when not compounded answers to *whose.*

Man is the impersonal pronoun, commonly translated with *one* or *we,* as *man kan ej,* one cannot, *hvad skall man göra?* what shall we do?

The rest of the pronouns are easily learnt by practice. I have only to add, that such as are compounded, are generally inflected as when single; thus the neuter gender of *hvarannan* is *hvarannat;* the genitive case of *hvar och en* is *hvars och ens,* &c.

Of the Numerals.

These are of two kinds, the Indefinite and Definite. The former (commonly called cardinal) leave the following noun in the indefinite state; the latter (or ordinal) require it to be definite 14)

14) Except when a pronoun is used before them, or when a noun,

as *en gång*, one time; *första gången*, first time; *sexton år*, sixteen years; *sextonde året*, sixteenth year.

The Indefinite or Cardinal.

En	1.	*Sexton*	16.
Två	2.	*Sjutton*	17.
Tre	3.	*Aderton*	18.
Fyra	4.	*Nitton*	19.
Fem	5.	*Tjugu*	20.
Sex	6.	*Tjuguen*	21.
Sju	7.	*Trettie*	30.
Åtta	8.	*Fyratie.*	40.
Nie 15)	9.	*Femtie*	50.
Tie	10.	*Sextie*	60.
Elfva	11.	*Sjuttie*	70.
Tolf	12.	*Åttatie*	80.
Tretton	13.	*Nittie*	90.
Fjorton	14.	*Hundra*	100.
Femton	15.	*Tusen*	1000.

The Definite or Ordinal.

Första	1st.	*Tredje*	3d.
Andra	2d.	*Fjerde*	4th.

pronoun or participle, that belongs to the same sentence, precedes them in the genitive case, as *i* mitt *sextonde år*, in my sixteenth year; Konungens *andre Son*, the Kings second Son; for in these cases the definite numerals are under the same rules as adjectives, (see the syntax) and leave the following substantive in the indefinite state.

15) We formerly wrote *nio, tio, tretio, fyratio*, which mode of writing is still frequently meth with. The above is however sanctioned by the best authority, and always used in speaking.

Femte	5th.	*Adertonde*	18th.
Sjette	6th.	*Nittonde*	19th.
Sjunde	7th.	*Tjugonde*	20th.
Åttonde	8th.	*Tjuguförsta*	21st.
Nionde	9th.	*Trettionde*	30th.
Tionde	10th.	*Fyrationde*	40th.
Elfte	11th.	*Femtionde*	50th.
Tolfte	12th.	*Sextionde*	60th.
Trettonde	13th.	*Sjuttionde*	70th.
Fjortonde	14th.	*Åttionde*	80th.
Femtonde	15th.	*Nittionde*	90th.
Sextonde	16th.	*Hundrade*	100th.
Sjuttonde	17th.	*Tusende*	1000th.

Of the AUXILIARY VERBS.

As all verbs both regular and irregular are in-flected by auxiliary ones, these should be particularly attended to. The following occur in the Swedish language.

At Hafva, to have.

Present tense.		Imperfect. tense.	
Singular.		*Singular.*	
Jag	I have.	*Jag*	I had.
Du } *hafver,*	thou hast.	*Du* } *hade,*	thou hadst.
Han } or *har,*	he has.	*Han* }	he had.
Plural.		*Plural.*	
Vi *hafva,* we		*Vi hade,* we	
J *hafven,* you } have.		*J haden,* you } had.	
De *hafva,* they		*De hade,* they	

Optative Mode.	Imperative Mode 16).

Singular.   *Singular.*

Hafve jag! may I
Hafve du! or thou } have.
Hafve han! migt he

Haf du, have thou.
lât honom hafva } let
     or   } him
Hafve han, } have

Plural.   *Plural.*

Hafvom vi! may we
Hafven J! or you } have.
Hafve de! might they

lât oss hafva, let us have.
Haf Ni or *hafven J,*
have you.   [have.
lât dem hafva, let them

Infinitive Mode.

At hafva.

Pres. particip. *hafvande*, having.
Preterite part. *haft*,   had.

16) It is not without some hesitation that I have stated the above forms of the Optative and Imperative modes, for as they are nearly allied both in signification and power, they seem to have been used one for the other, or rather, to have constituted but one mode. Besides this I do not recollect to have observed *all* the persons of the Optative Mode being used by our writers, and may therefore be mistaken, when I say, that the present genius of the language requires them. As to the Imperative Mode, the second person sing. is in all verbs not only decidedly expressed, but also different from the Optative; but the third person sing. and the second plur. which last I have stated to be the same as the second sing. appear commonly in the Optative forms; and I have therefore retained both constructions, submitting however to better judges the whole of the above, which, as a prototype, I have followed throughout this work.

At Vara, to be (esse).

Present tense.	Imperfect tense.
Singular.	*Singular.*
Jag, du, han, är, I am, &c.	*Jag, du, han, var,* I was, &c.
Plural.	*Plural.*
Vi äro, we ⎫	*Vi voro,* we ⎫
J ären, you ⎬ are.	*J voren,* you ⎬ were.
De äro, they ⎭	*De voro,* they ⎭

Subjunctive Mode.	Optative Mode.
Singular.	*Singular.*
Jag, du, han, vore, I were, &c.	*Vare Jag, du, han!*
Plural.	*Plural.*
Vi vore, we ⎫	*Varom vi!*
J voren, you ⎬ were.	*Varen J!*
De vore, they ⎭	*Vare de!*

Imperative Mode.	Infinitive Mode.
Var du, be thou.	*At vara.*
låt honom vara, or	Pres. part. *varande,* being.
Vare han, &c.	Preter. part. *varit,* been.

At Varda and *at Blifva*, to be (become).

Present tense.	Imperfect tense.
Singular.	*Singular.*
Jag ⎫	*Jag* ⎫
Du ⎬ *varder.*	*Du* ⎬ *vardt.*
Han ⎭	*Han* ⎭
Plural	*Plural.*
Vi varda.	*Vi vordo.*
J varden.	*J vorden.*
De varda.	*De vordo.*

Subjunctive Mode.

Singular.

Jag, du, han vorde.

Plural.

Vi vorde.

J vorden.

De vorde.

Optative Mode.

Singular.

Varde jag, du, han!

Plural.

Vardom vi!

Varden J!

Varde de!

Imperative Mode.

Varde.

låt honom varda, or

Varde han, &c.

Infinitive Mode.

At varda.

Pres. act. part. *vardande*

Pret. act. part. *vartit* (obsolete).

Pres. pass. part. *vorden*, n. *vordet*.

Pres. tense.	Imperf. tense.	Subjunctive mode.
Sing.	*Sing.*	*Sing.*
Jag	Jag	Jag, du, han blefve.
Du } blifver 17)	Du } blef.	*Plur.*
Han } or blir.	Han }	Vi blefve.
Plur.	*Plur.*	J blefven.
Vi blifva.	Vi blefvo.	De blefve.
J blifven.	J blefven.	
De blifva.	De blefvo.	

17) *Jag blifver* and *jag varder* are translated *I be, I will be, I be-come, I grow*, according as the meaning of the sentence may require; as *om jag blifver hemma*, if I be at home; *han varder kommande*, he will be coming; *han vardt stor*, he became great; *han blef fet*, he grew fat, &c. The verb *blifver* may also denote to remain, as *Jag blifver här*, I remain here; but practice will soon teach the different use and significations of these verbs.

Optative mode.	Imperative mode.
Blifve jag, du, han!	*Blif.*
Blifvom vi!	*låt honom blifva*, or
Blifven J!	*Blifve han, &c.*
Blifve de!	

Infinitive mode.
At blifva.

Present act. part. *blifvande.*

Pret. act. part. *blifvit.*

Pres. pass. part. *blifven*, neutr. *blifvet.*

Obs. a. The future tense of these and all other verbs is expressed by *skall*, as *Jag, Du, Han skall hafva, Vi skole, J skolen, De skola varda.*

b. The conjunctive and potential modes have the following characteristics: *Jag må, jag tör,* I may; *Jag måtte, jag torde,* I might; *Jag kan, jag kunde,* (of the verb *at kunna*, to be able) *jag måste,* I must; *Jag skulle,* I should; *Jag bör, jag borde,* I ought, &c.

c. As the verb *at vilja (jag vill, jag ville,* I will, I would) indicates rather an absolute volition in the Swedish language, we use another when the case is not positive, viz *lärer*, as *Han lärer komma,* he will or may (probably) come. *Han vill komma,* would be, he is inclined, or he wishes to come.

d. *At göra*, to do, is a substitute verb in the Swedish language used (as pronouns in similar cases for nouns) to avoid the repetition of the preceding verb, as *skrifver du?* do you write? *Ja gör jag,* yes I do, instead of *Ja jag skrifver.* But it is never put before other verbs as a sign of a tense; We cannot say, *Jag gör gå, han gjorde se,* (I do go, he did see) as *do* and *did* are used in the English.

Of the Regular Verbs.

All such verbs end in the infinitive mode with *a,* and may be divided into three 18) conjugations. The 1st ends in the pres. tense in *ar,* in the imp. in *ade.*

The 2d — — — — — *er,* — — *de.*

The 3d — — — — — *er,* — — *te.*

as will appear from the following paradigms.

First Conjugation.

At Hata, to hate.

Present tense.	Imperf. tense.	Perfect tense.
Singular.		*Jag hafver hatat.*
Jag	*Jag*	Pluperf. tense.
Du }*hatar.*	*Du* }*hatade.*	*Jag hade hatat.*
Han	*Han*	Future tense.
Plural.		*Jag skall hata.*
Vi hata.	*Vi hatade.*	
J haten.	*J hataden.*	
De hata.	*De hatade.*	

18) The Swedish Language might well be said to have but one regular conjugation, considering that more than three fourths of the verbs are inflected after the *first,* and that a great number which now have *de* and *te* in the imperfect tense, were formerly there ended in *ade.*

Potential Mode.

Jag
Du } må, I may hate.
Han

Jag måtte, I might,
Jag måste, I must,
Jag skulle I should
hata, or hate, or
hafva hatat, have hated.
&c. &c. &c. &c.

Vi måga
J mågen } or må hata.
De måga

Jag
Du } kan, I can hate.
Han

Jag
Du } kunde I could
Han } hata, hate, &c.

Vi kunna
J kunnen } hata.
De kunna

Vi kunde
J kunden } hata.
De kunde

Optative mode.

Hate Jag, Du, Han!
may or might I hate, &c.
Hatom vi!
Haten J!
Hate de!

Imperative mode.

Hata du, hate thou.
låt honom hata, or hate
låt oss hata.   {han.
Hata Ni, or haten J.
låt dem hata.

Infinitive Mode.

At hata, to hate.

Pres. part. hatande, hating.

Pret. part. hatat,   hated.

The Active verbs are formed into Passives, by the addition of an s, in the following manner:

At Hatas, to be hated.

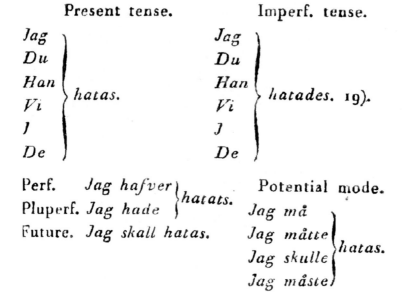

Present tense.		Imperf. tense.	
Jag		*Jag*	
Du		*Du*	
Han	} *hatas.*	*Han*	} *hatades.* 19).
Vi		*Vi*	
J		*J*	
De		*De*	

Perf. *Jag hafver* } *hatats.*
Pluperf. *Jag hade*
Future. *Jag skall hatas.*

Potential mode.

Jag må
Jag måtte } *hatas.*
Jag skulle
Jag måste

Optative Mode.

Må or *måtte jag, du, han, &c. hatas.*

Imperative Mode.

Låt mig, dig, honom, &c. hatas.

19) The persons of the passive verbs, in the present and imperfect tenses, are not distinguished by their terminations, as those of the active, (In this conjugation even the singular and plural numbers are alike). The regular form of the second person in plural occurs however, as *J hatens, J hatadens;* but then it does not strictly mean, you are or were hated, but rather, you hate or hated each other. The same does the optative (regular) form *hatoms, hatens* indicate, as *hatens J!* may you hate one another! and it is therefore generally expressed by *må,* or *måtte,* as *må jag hatas!* may I be hated! *måtte jag höras!* O that I might be heard! The others, as well as *J hatens* and *J hatadens* seem to be reciprocal forms.

Infinitive Mode.

At hatas, to be hated.

Pres. part. 20) *hatad*, neutr. *hatadt*, hated.
Pret. part. *hatats*, been hated.

Second Conjugation.

At Värma, to warm.

Jag		Jag		Perf. Jag hafver	
Du	värmer.	Du	värmde.	Ppf. Jag hade	värmt
Han		Han		Fut. Jag skall	
Vi värma.		Vi värmde.		Jag må	värma
J värmen.		J värmden.		Jag skulle	
De värma.		De värmde.			

Optative Mode.	Imperative Mode.
Värme jag, du, han!	*Värm du,* warm thou.
may or might I warm &c.	*låt honom värma.*
Värmom vi!	*låt oss värma.*
Värmen J!	*Värm Ni,* or *värmen J.*
Värme de!	*låt dem värma.*

Infinitive

20) This participle in all verbs belonging to this conjugation, is (as present participles in general) also used as an adjective, but suffers no inflection in the degrees of comparison, which are distinguished by *mer, mindre, mest, minst.* Observe here also, that the *present active participle* sometimes appears in the passive form, *as hatandes;* but as it still, when used absolute, retains an active signification, it cannot with propriety be called a passive participle. I would rather give it the name of an Active *Gerund;* but when it has before it the preposition *til* (to), as *det är til fruktandes,* it is to be feared, I would, as it then has a passive sense, call it a Passive *Gerund;* but these two forms seldom occur.

Infinitive Mode.

At värma.

Pres. part. *värmande,* warming.

Pret. part. *värmt,* warmed.

The Passive. *At värmas,* to be warmed

Present tense.	Imperfect tense.
Jag, du, han värmes.	*Jag, du, han* } *värmdes.*
Vi, J, de värmas.	*Vi, J, de* }
I am warmed, &c.	I was warmed, &c.

Perf. *Jag hafver* } *värmts.* *Jag må* }

Pperf. *Jag hade* } *Jag måtte* } *värmas.*

Fut. *Jag skall värmas.* *Jag skulle, &c.* }

Optative Mode.

Må or *måtte jag, &c. värmas!*

Imperative Mode.

Låt mig, dig, honom, oss, &c. värmas.

Infinitive Mode.

At värmas.

Pres. part. *värmd,* neutr. *värmdt,* warmed.

Pret. part. *värmts,* been warmed.

Third Conjugation.

At Söka, to seek.

Present tense.	Imperfect tense.
Jag } *söker.*	*Jag* } *sökte.*
Du }	*Du* }
Han }	*Han* }
I seek, &c.	I sought, &c.

Vi söka.　　　　　　　*Vi sökte.*

J söken.　　　　　　　*J sökten.*

De söka.　　　　　　　*De sökte.*

Perf. *Jag hafver*⎫　　*Jag skall*　　　⎫

Pperf. *Jag hade* ⎬*sökt.*　*Jag må* 　　　⎬*söka.*

　　　　　　　　　　　Jag måste, &c.⎭

Optative mode.　　　　Imperative mode.

Söke jag, du, han!　　*Sök du,* seek thou.

may or might I seek.　　*låt honom söka.*

Sökom vi!　　　　　　*låt oss söka.*

Söken J!　　　　　　*Sök Ni,* or *söken J.*

Söke de!　　　　　　*låt dem söka.*

Infinitive mode.

At söka.

Pres. part. *sökande,* seeking.

Pret. part. *sökt,* sought.

The Passive. *At Sökas,* to be sought.

Present tense.　　　　Imperfect tense.

Jag, du, han sökes.　　*Jag, du, han*⎫

Vi, J, de sökas.　　　*Vi, J, de* 　⎬*söktes.*

I am sought, &c.　　　I was sought, &c.

Perf. *Jag hafver*⎫　　*Jag skall* 　⎫

Pperf. *Jag hade* ⎬*sökts.*　*Jag må, &c.*⎬*sökas.*

Optative mode.

Må, or *måtte jag, &c. sökas!*

Imperative mode.

Låt mig, dig, honom, oss, &c. sökas.

Infinitive mode.

At sökas.

Present part. *sökt* 21) sought.

Preter. part. *sökts*, been sought.

Of the DEMI-PASSIVES.

Verbs in the Swedish language that have a passive termination, and either active or neuter signification, I call Demi-Passives. Such are of
The First Conjugation 22) *At Hoppas*, to hope.
The Second — — — *At Trifvas*, to thrive.
The Third — — — *At Synas*,   to appear.

Obs. These are all inflected as Passives; but not being passive in signification, they have only the Active Participles, which however are constructed as passive with an *s*, as *hoppandes, hoppats; trifvandes, trifts; synandes, synts.* We can never say *hoppad, trifd, synt*, which would be the Passive Participles.

Of the IRREGULAR VERBS.

Of these there is a considerable number in the Swedish as well as in other languages. To bring them all under certain classes would be altogether impossible, unless we extend the number of classes

---

21) The regular form of this Participle is in masc. and fem. *sökd* neutr. *sökdt*, but it is seldom observed, on account of the difficulty of pronouncing *d* after *k*.

22) Of these the same observation may be made as of the verbs of the *first* Conjugation, viz. that their number greatly exceeds the rest.

too far, as many of them would constitute a class
of their own; and to enumerate and minutely exa-
mine them all, would stretch this work beyond its
limits. I will therefore content myself with taking
into consideration those of the principal orders
only, and briefly mention the rest.

First Class.
At Finna, to find.

Verbs of this class end the present tense in *er*,
jag springer, I run: change the vowel into *a* and
become monosyllabic in the imperfect, *jag sprang*,
I ran, and end the active preterite participle in *it*,
after changing the vowel into *u*, *sprungit*, run, and
the present passive participle in *en*, neutr. *et*, *sprun-
gen*, *sprunget*, run. These seem to bear the greatest proportion to the rest. *Simma*, swim; *Brista*,
burst; *Brinna*, burn; *Vinna*, win; *Skära*, cut; *Stjäla*
steal; (imperf. *stal* part. *stulit*, *stulen*, neutr. *stulet*),
Bära, bear; *Sticka*, sting, &c. are all of this class,
and are inflected as follows:

Present tense.	Imperfect tense.
Jag, du, han finner.	*Jag, du, han fann.*
Vi finna. I find, &c.	*Vi funno.* I found, &c.
J finnen.	*J funnen.*
De finna.	*De funno.*

Perf. *Jag hafver*⎫
Pperf. *Jag hade* ⎬ *funnit.*
Fut. *Jag skall finna.*

Potent mode.	Optative mode.	Imp. mode.

Jag må ⎫
Jag måtte ⎪
Jag skulle ⎬ *finna.*
Jag måste, ⎪
&c. ⎭

Finne jag! &c. Finn du, find thou.
may I find, &c. *låt honom finna.*
Finnom vi! *låt oss finna.*
Finnen J! *Finn Ni,* or *finnen J.*
Finne de! *låt dem finna.*

Infinitive mode.

At finna, to find.

Pres. part. *finnande,* finding.
Pret. part. *funnit,* found.

Obs. Verbs of this class, that bear to be passively explained, are also inflected as such, whilst those that are neuter (ex. gr. *brista, brinna*) do not admit of a passive inflection, except in the present participle, which they seem to have in common with all the rest: Thus we hear it said, *Isen är brusten,* the ice is burst; *Huset är brunnet,* the house is burnt, &c.

The Passive. *At finnas,* to be found.

Pres. tense.	Imperf. tense.	Perfect.

Jag ⎫
Du ⎬ *finnes,* am found.
Han ⎭

Jag ⎫
Du ⎬ *fans,* was found.
Han ⎭

Jag hafver ⎫
P. perf. ⎬ *funnits.*
Jag hade ⎭

Vi finnas. *Vi funnos.* Fut.

J finnens. *J funnens.* *Jag skall finnas.*

De finnas. *De funnos.*

Jag må, måtte, skulle, måste, kan, kunde, &c. finnas.

Optative mode.

Må or *måtte jag &c. finnas.*

(The regular form)

Finnes jag, du, han!

Finnoms vi!

Finnens J! 23)

Finnes de!

Imperative mode.

Låt mig, dig, honom, &c. finnas.

Infinitive mode.

At finnas.

Pres. part. *funnen,* neutr. *funnet,* found.

Pret. part. *funnits,* been found.

Second Class.

At Bita, to bite.

Verbs of this class end the present tense as those of the first, *jag biter,* I bite: change the vowel into *e* and become monosyllabic in the imperfect, *jag bet,* I bit: end the active pret. participle in *it, bitit,* bit, and the present passive participle in *en* neutr. *et, biten, bitet,* bitten. These are inflected after the preceding paradigm, with this difference, that the original vowel (or that of the root, which in *bita* is *i*) is never changed into *u,* as it is in

23) The second person plural of the present and imperfect tenses, and the 1st and 2d plural of the optative mode, which in regular passives are rather reciprocal, (see note 19 p. 51) are not strictly so in the irregular, where consequently the above inflections appear to be used with propriety.

those of the first class; thus in the imperfect plural
we say *beto* not *buto*, and in the preterit participle
butit not *butit*. *Skrifva*, write (*skref*, wrote; *skrifvit, skrifven, skrifvet*, written) *drifva*, drive; *rida*,
ride; *gråta*, weep; *klifva*, climb; *vrida*, writhe,
(and others to a considerable number) are all of
this class.

Obs. Besides these two principal classes, that
change the vowel in the imperfect tense into *a* and
e, there are others that change it into *o*, *å*, or *ö*;
but of these I shall make no separate classes, their
number being but small. The following may serve
for examples.

1st. Such as change the vowel into *u* (like those
of the first class) in the participles.

Infinit. mode. Imp. T. Pret. act. Pres. pass. part.
part.

Svära, to swear. *svor, svurit, svuren*, n. *svuret.*
Frysa, to freeze. *frös, frusit, frusen*, n. *fruset.*
Skjuta, to shoot. *sköt, skjutit, skjuten*, n. *skjutet.*
Knyta, to knit. *knöt, knutit, knuten*, n. *knutet.*

Obs. Those that have *ö* in the imperfect tense
differ from the first class, in not changing that *ö*
into *u* in plural, as *jag, du, han frös, vi fröso,
J frösen, de fröso*, not *fruso, frusen, fruso.*

2dly. Such as are like those of the Second Class.

Infinit M. Imp. T. Pt. a. p. Pres. pass. part.
Draga, to draw. *drog, dragit, dragen*, n. *draget.*

Taga, to take. *tog*, *tagit*, *tagen*, n. *taget*.
Äta, to eat. *åt*, *ätit*, *äten*, n. *ätet*.
Hålla, to hold. *höll*, *hållit*, *hållen*, n. *hållet*.

Third Class.

At Se, to see.

Monosyllabic verbs 24) that remain so both in the imperfect tense (in which the vowel is changed) and the preterite participle, belong to this class. They all end, as verbs in general, with a vowel, and form the present active tense by adding an *r* to the infinitive mode; as *jag ser*, I see; and the passive (if they can be so expressed) by adding an *s*, as *jag ses*, I am seen. The pres. pass. participle, which, in verbs of the two preceding classes, is ended with *en*, neutr. *et;* these end with *dd*, neutr. *dt: sedd*, n, *sedt*, seen, and in the plural number of the imperfect tense, they do not change the vowel, but retain it as those of the second class.

Infin. M.	Imperf. tense.	Pt. a. p.	Pres. pass. part.
Se, see.	*såg*, pl. *sågo*,	*sett*,	*sedd*, neutr. *sedt*.
Gå. go.	*gick*, pl. *gingo*,	*gått*.	
Få, get.	*fick*, pl. *fingo*,	*fått*.	
Stå, stand.	*stod*, pl. *stodo*,	*stått*.	
Le, smile.	*log*, pl. *logo*,	*lett*.	

Obs. a. The present active participle, which

---

24) Some of these belong to the second Regular Conjugation, and are distinguished by the termination *de* being added to the infinitive mode to make the imperfect tense, when the letter *d* is always doubled, as *at så*, to sow, imperf. *sådde* not *såde*.

in other verbs is formed by adding *nde* to the infinitive mode, these form by adding *ende*, as se*ende*, seeing; gå*ende*, going, &c.

b. The imperfect plurals of *gå* and *få* (*gingo*, *fingo*) euphony seems to have introduced instead of *gicko, ficko*, after the German *ging*.

c. The present pass. participle of *gå, få, stå, le*, (*gådd*, n. *gådt; fådd*, n. *fådt; stådd*, n *stådt; ledd*, n. *ledt*) I have not expressed above, as not generally introduced. They occur however sometimes either singly or compounded; thus we will hear it said, *Den vägen är* gådd *på en dag*, that road is walked in a day; *Det är* fådt *för godt köp*, it is got at a low price; *Straffet är* utstådt, the punishment is over (stood out); *Han är* åtledd or ledd *åt*, he is laughed at. Obs. Instead of *gådd* and *gådt*, we use more *gången* and *gånget*.

Fourth Class.

Under this head I include all the rest of the irregular verbs, whatever be their anomaly. The undermentioned are such as occur most frequently, and may serve for examples. Some of them being real actives are also passively inflected. Thus for instance, *at lägga, sätta* and *bedja* have a passive infinitive, *at läggas, sättas, bedjas*, as well as other inflections, which practice must teach. I here only give the Infinitive mode, the Present and Imperfect tenses, and the Preterite Active Participle.

Inf. mode.	Pres. tense.	Impf. tense.	Pret. a. part.
At Bedja, to beg.	*Jag beder,* or *ber,*	*Jag bad,*	*bedit* or *bedt.*
At Bjuda, to bid.	*Jag bjuder,*	*Jag bjöd,*	*bjudit.*
At Bringa, to bring.	*Jag bringar,*	*Jag bragte,*	*bragt.*
At Böra,	*Jag bör,* I ought,	*Jag borde,*	*bort.*
At Heta, to be called.	*Jag heter* *),	*Jag hette,*	*hetat.*
At Komma, to come.	*Jag kommer,*	*Jag kom,*	*kommit.*
At Kunna, to be able.	*Jag kan,*	*Jag kunde,*	*kunnat.*
At Ligga, to lie.	*Jag ligger,*	*Jag låg,* lay,	*legat.*
At Lägga, to lay.	*Jag lägger,*	*Jag lade,*	*lagt.*
At Sitta, to sit.	*Jag sitter,*	*Jag satt,*	*setat* or *sutit.*
At Sjunga, to sing.	*Jag sjunger,*	*Jag sjöng,*	*sjungit.*
At Sjunka, to sink.	*Jag sjunker,*	*Jag sjönk* 25),	*sjunkit.*

*) *Jag heter Anders,* my name is Andrew; *hvad heter det?* what is it called?

25) The imperfect tense of *sjunga* and *sjunka* (as well as the participles) appears sometimes without the j, as *söng, sönk; sungen, sunken;* and some will even (though very improperly) write *sang* and *sank.*

At Sätta,   *Jag sätter,*   *Jag satte,*   *satt.*
to set.

At Veta,   *Jag vet,*   *Jag viste,*   *vetat.*
to know.

At Vilja,   *Jag vill,*   *Jag ville,*   *velat.*
to will.

At Växa,   *Jag växer,*   *Jag växte, växt* or
to grow.   *vuxit.*

Of the Demi-Passives there are also a few irregular, which may be referred to this class, as

Infin. mode.   Pres. tense.   Imp. tense.   Prt. part.

At Vederfaras, *det vederfares, vederfors, vederfa-*
to befal.   *rits.*

At Förgås,   *Jag förgås,*   *förgicks,*   *förgåtts.*
to perish.

At Umgås.   *Jag umgås,*   *umgicks,*   *umgåtts.*
to hold intercourse with.

At Brås (på), *Jag brås,*   *bråddes,*   *bråtts.*
to take after, to resemble.

Exercises on the Verbs.

The learner should endeavour to translate the following constructions into English, as in understanding a language, and correctly speaking the same, much depends on being well acquainted with the different forms and inflections of the verbs.

Jag har varit. Du har blifvit. Han skall varda. De skulle hafva. Du måste vara. Vi hade haft.

'Jag torde komma. Du varder stor. De vordo glade. Han skulle hafva varit. Hon måtte hafva haft. Du måste varda hatad. Han måste vara hatad. Jag kan blifva glad. Du må vara hög. Det har blifvit stort. Det är blifvet stort. Jag skulle hafva hatat. Måtte jag hafva kunnat. Du torde blifva gifven. Han skall kunna göra. Jag hatas och fruktas. Om de vorde. Vi alle hatades. Du skulle hafva hatats. Det vardt hatadt. Det blef värmdt. Blifve du värmd! Söke han oss! Värme de sig! Han har värmts. Jag tör kunna värmas. De torde kunna sökas. Kunde det finnas? Har du funnit det? Har det blifvit funnet? Det har funnits. Finnes han lycklig! (happy). Måtte han varda funnen! De funnos glade. Viljen J hafva sett? De torde hafva skrifvit. Skrifve de til mig! Det skulle hafva skrifvits. De skrefvos. Det måste hafva blifvit skrifvet. Måtte du hafva sjungit! De sjöngo väl. Jag borde hafva satt mig. Du borde hafva sutit. Han skulle sätta sig. Blif sittande. Måste du veta det? Han viste at jag har vetat det. Jag måste hafva förgåtts. Du hade varit förgången. De förgingos alla. Han brås på sin fader. Hans broder borde hafva bråtts på honom. Jag umgås icke der. Han umgicks med mig. Vi umgingos alla dagar.

Of the PARTICLES.

The particles are commonly admitted to be of

four kinds, viz. Adverbs, Conjunctions, Prepositions, and Interjections.

An Adverb is a part of speech joined to other
words to express the quality or circumstances of
them; and as these vary, the adverbs of course
are of different kinds. Some have relation to *time*,
others to *place, probability, doubt, quantity*, &c.
as *nu*, now; *hemma*, at home; *här*, here; *troligen*,
likely; *om*, if; *mycket*, much, &c.

Of the adverbs a few admit of comparison, as
ofta, often, *oftare, oftast; fort*, quickly, *fortare,
fortast; endels*, partly, *merendels, mestadels*.

When adjectives are used as adverbs (and
many of them are) they appear always in the neuter
gender, as *naturligt*, naturally; *högt*, highly; *has-
tigt*, hastily; and sometimes adverbs are formed
from them by adding *ligen*, as *högligen, storligen*.
If the adjectives end with *lig*, (as *naturlig*) only *en*
are added, as *naturligen, skamligen*, shamefully, &c.

Conjunctions join words and sentences together, as *och*, and; *ock*, also; *nemligen*, namely;
men, but; *eller*, or; *antingen*, either; *hvarken*,
neither; *ty*, for; *ehuru*, although, &c.

The prepositions are words set before nouns
or pronouns, to express the relations of persons,
places, and things to each other, as *jag bör gå
til honom*, I ought to go *to* him; such are *under*,
under; *öfver*, over; *på* and *uppå*, on or upon;
efter, after; *från*, from: *i* and *uti*, in, &c.

Of the Interjections or words that express any
sudden emotion of the mind, from the sensation
either of pleasure or pain, the following are the
most common: *O! ack!* O! alas! *ha!* (exclamation
of despair) *hu!* (of horror) *aj!* (of pain) *si!* lo!
ve! wo! *hå!* ho! *fy!* fie! &c.

THE SYNTAX *a*).

The Common Swedish Alphabet.

As many Swedish books, &c. are printed with
these letters, the learner should make himself well
acquainted with them, so as to be able to know
them distinctly, whenever they occur.

The Capital Letters.

𝔄	A	ℌ	H	𝔓	P	𝔚	W
𝔅	B	ℑ	I	𝔔	Q	𝔛	X
ℭ	C	𝔎	K	𝔑	R	𝔜	Y
𝔇	D	𝔏	L	𝔖	S	𝔷	Z
𝔈	E	𝔐	M	𝔗	T	𝔄̊	Å
𝔉	F	𝔑	N	𝔘	U	𝔄̈	Ä
𝔊	G	𝔒	O	𝔙	V	𝔒̈	Ö

a) Taking for granted (as I have done throughout this work) that
the reader knows the grammar of his own language, I deem it
superfluous to be minute on this head; and consequently passing
over such rules as the two languages acknowledge in common, I
will here only state some material points in which they disagree,
and occasionally hint at such singularities, as without an explanation, would be difficult for a beginner.

The Small and Compounded Letters.

ɑ	a	ſ	l	ʋ	v	ffi	ffi
b	b	m	m	w	w	ffl	ffl
c	c	n	n	ʒ	x	ft	fi.
d	d	o	o	y	y	ſſ	ſl
e	e	p	p	ʒ	z	ſl	ll
f	f	q	q	å	å	ſi	ſi
g	g	r	r	ä	ä	ſl	ſl
h	h	ſ	ſ	ö	ö	ff	ff
i	i	s	s	ch	ch	ſs	ſs
j	j	t	t	ck	ck	ſt	ſt
k	k	u	u	ff	ff	tz	tz

For the sounds of the different letters I refer the learner to the beginning of this work. The order they here stand in is that of the Swedish Alphabet. The compounded letters are added, that, when seen separately, they may be the better distinguished in reading.

On Pronunciation.

When the Alphabet is known, the changeable consonants and their different sounds before the *hard* and the *soft* vowels (see page 7) should be carefully attended to, as upon this chiefly a correct pronunciation depends, and in order to acquire it, the root of the word must be examined, for just as the sound of these consonants is there heard, so it remains through all inflections: Thus, for instance, *g* in *ring* retains its original sound (the same as *g* in the English word *ring*) both in the plural number *ringar*, and with the definite article *ringen*: *g* in *tänger*, tongs, has the same sound as in the singular *tång*: *k* in *söker* the same as in the infinitive mode *söka*: *sk* in *asken* the same as in *ask*, box, &c.; for these *(ar, en, er)* are only nominal or verbal terminations, which, as they do not belong to the same syllable as the changeable consonants, have no influence on their sound; but if the vowel of the *radix* be changed into another, (as is often the case in the irregular verbs) then the sound of these consonants changes at the same time; for instance, *sk* in *skära*, to cut, have a soft sound, but in the imperfect tense *skar* they become hard, as *ä* is there changed into *a*.

In a few words, adopted from the French, *ch* retain their foreign sound, as *charm*, *chocolad*, pronounce sjarm, sjoklad; the same do *g* in *j* in *geni*, *jurnal*, *läckage*, &c. pronounce sjeni, sjurnal, läckasje. Obs. Foreign words were formerly spelt as in those languages from which they were borrowed; but we now conform the spelling to the genius of our own; thus we write *Kusin*, *Mamsell*, *Löjtnant*, instead of Cousin, Mademoiselle, Lieutenant, &c.

As the sound of *g*, *k*, and *sk* becomes hard before the hard vowels, we find a *j* added when they
require

require a soft sound: *g* in *göra*, for instance, would in the imperfect tense lose its soft sound before the hard *o*, if *j* was not inserted; we therefore write *gjorde* (not gorde), because we pronounce it so *b*). In the same manner *j* is added after *sk* in *skjuta*, to shoot; *skjorta*, shirt, &c.

Again, when *j* is found in a word before a hard vowel, (whereby the changeable consonants get a soft sound) it is generally left out as superfluous when a soft vowel follows: Thus we write the imperfect tense of the verb *skjuta*, *sköt* not *skjöt*, because *sk* before *ö* by themselves sound as *skj*, or as the English *sh*.

When a word, that is not monosyllabic, ends with a vowel, we may generally conclude that such vowels constitute either a nominal or verbal termination: Thus we should properly spell *böna*, bean, *bön-a*, *yx-a*, axe; *pål-e*, pole; *fiend-e*, fiend; *törn-e*, thorn; *hjert-a*, heart; *hammar-e*, hammer; and the infinitive mode of the verbs thus: *äsk-a*, to ask; *värm-a*, to warm; *sätt-a*, to set; *sök-a*, to seek; *sitt-a*, to sit; *drag-a*, to draw, &c. This appears quite clear when we observe how the same

---

b) Some spell for the same reason *menniska*, (human being, man or woman), plur. *menniskor* with a *j*, *menniskja*, *menniskjor*, which mode of spelling, as it is consonant with the present genius of the language, I would prefer, if the best authority had not long admitted this word to be an exception.

words are written in the others dialects of the old Gothic language, and the examples I have here given, may partly serve to prove, how nearly allied the Swedish is to the English, as also, that the final vowel is only a modification of the original word, or as I have called it before, a nominal or verbal termination; but what proves this still more is, that the changeable consonants, when placed before such terminations, do not alter their sound, but retain it the same as in the original word; and thus we see the reason, why *g, k*, and *sk*, when followed by *e*, (or any other of the soft vowels) often have a hard sound, as in *båge*, bow; *märke*, mark; *buske*, bush, not *bågje, märkje, buskje*, because the word originally is *båg-e, märk-e, busk-e*, and not *bå-ge, mär-ke, bu-ske*.

What has here been said of the final vowels, relates also to the other nominal or verbal terminations. In Verbs the following occur with a soft vowel: *e, it, en, et, its*, as in the word *drag-a*, to draw; *drag-e!* (the optative mode); *dragit*, (pret. act. partic.); *dragen, draget, dragits*, (the passive participles); and consequently we do not read *dragje, dragjit, dragjen, dragjet, dragjits*, but pronounce the *g* as in *draga*.

In Nouns, besides the plural termination *er* of the third declension, these two must be observed, viz. *else* and *eri*, as *helgelse*, sanctification; *bak-*

else, pastry *c*); pronounce here *g* and *k*, as in *helga*, to sanctify; *baka*, to bake; and in *bryggeri*, brewery; *dykeri*, diving company; *fiskeri*, fishery, as in *brygga*, to brew; *dyka*, to dive; *fiska*, to fish.

As to the termination *el* in *nagel*, nail; *kakel*, glazed brick; *muskel*, muscle, &c. the *e* seems here inserted to assist in pronouncing *l* (in the same manner as we now write *vatten*, water, for *vatn*) and to prevent the preceding consonant from sounding double (see page 9, note 4, b.), and it has therefore no influence on *g*, *k*, and *sk*, in such words.

In Adjectives the terminations *en*, neutr. *et*, and *ig*, neutr. *igt*, are, among those beginning with a soft vowel, the most common, as *trogen*, faithful; *sniken*, covetous; *vågig*, wavy; *krokig*, crooked; *buskig*, bushy, &c. pronounce *trog-en*, *snik-en*, *våg-ig*, *krok-ig*, *busk-ig*.

The *e* in the termination *elig*, neutr. *eligt*, begins more and more to be laid aside; thus we now write *odräglig*, insupportable; *ömklig*, pitiable; *älsklig*, dear; instead of *odrägelig*, *ömkelig*, *älskelig*, and if it should be expressed, it has no influence on the changeable consonants. Obs. *g* in

---

c) *sk* occur never before the terminations *else* (*öfverraskelse*, surprise; *vaskelse*, washing, &c. barbarous words); nor before *en* in the adjectives, (*tresken*, stubborn, and others are obsolete, we now write *tresk*, &c.); and that they cannot be followed by *isk*, euphony alone will tell.

talgig, besmeared with tallow; *sorglig*, sorrowful, &c. sounds as *j;* but this is no exception, for it is here pronounced as in the primitive words *talg, sorg*, (see page 8, letter g.)

Adjectives have also a termination *isk*, as in *krigisk*, warlike; *grekisk*, greek, when *g* and *k* must be heard as in the root of the word, or as in *krig*, war; *Grek*, a Greek.

Of the *e* final, with which adjectives appear both in the plural number and in the definite state, as *höge*, high; *rake*, straight; *friske*, sound, &c. I deem it superfluous to say any thing here, as it is comprehended in what I have already observed on the final vowels.

On the accentuation of the words, the following general rules should be attended to.

Monosyllabic words, ending with a double consonant, or with a consonant that has a double sound, or with two consonants, of which the former sounds double (see note 4, page 9), are pronounced *short*, as *all, hatt, aj, vax, som, verk;* the others, as well as those ending with a vowel *long*, as *ek*, oak; *tog*, took; *gå*, go; *se*, see. NB Add to the monosyllabics in *n*, (mentioned in page 9, note 4, d.), the article *en*, neutr. *et*, and also the numeral *en*, one, which last for the sake of distinction appears in the neuter gender with *tt (ett)*.

Obs. The addition of *t* in the neuter gender does not make the adjective sound short; thus we pronounce *fult* not *fullt* of *ful*, ugly; *sent* not *sennt*, of *sen*, late; but if the adjective ends with *d* or *t*, it is pronounced *short*, as otherwise the *t* of the neuter gender could not distinctly be heard, as *gladt*, *fett*, of *glad; fet*, fat.

Words, consisting of two syllables, have the accent on the first *d*). Thus, for instance, the *a* final in all verbs is *short*, as in *hata, söka, springa*. And where the accent is in the root, there it remains in the inflections: *hätade, hätande, pēnningar*, have the first syllable *long*, because it is so in *hāta* and *pēnning*.

Words, consisting of three syllables, have also

d) Except. 1. All words beginning with the inseparable particle *be* as *bestå*, to consist; *begå*, to commit, which have the accent on the last.

2. Nouns (and these are very few) ending in *as* and *os*, as *kalas*, banquet; *matros*, sailor; have always the accent on those syllables, and retain it so through all inflections.

3. Words adopted from foreign languages (as also nominal nouns ending with *an* and *in*) have all the accent on the last, as in *fatal, planet, pistol, parti, Spartan, Dalin*.

4. Words beginning with *för*, and deriving their signification chiefly from that preposition, as *förman*, foreman; *fördom*, prejudice, &c. have always the accent on the first syllable But when *för* has no decided signification, (as when it answers to *for* in the English) it is never accentuated; thus in *förgås*, to perish; *förstå*, to understand, the stress must be laid on *å*. This observation relates also to words of more than two syllables: In *försaka*, to forsake; *förgäta*, to forget; *försvära*, to forswear, &c. *för* is not accentuated, but in *förmiddag*, forenoon, *förberedelse*, preparation, &c, it is so for the reason assigned.

the accent on the first *e*), as *skräddare*, taylor; *fiende*, enemy; *vetenskap*, science, &c.

Words, consisting of more than three syllables, are variously accentuated. In general it may be remarked, that they have the accent as much forward as possible; Thus the words *kūnungarne*, *penningarne*, *vidskepelse*, superstition, have it on the *first;* the same have all, beginning with a preposition or particle (except *be* and *för*), as *genomvandra*, to pervade; *mellankomma*, to intervene; *anförare*, leader, &c.; but if they be lengthened through inflections, as *genomvandrande*, *mellankommande*, the first syllable both of the preposition and of the original word sounds *long*, which is the case also in other compounded words, as in *andaktsöfning*, devotion; *arbetskammare*, workshop; *ickedessmindre*, nevertheless, &c.

Obs. Words ending with *i* and *inna*, as also verbs in *era*, and their derivatives, have the accent as stated in the note below *e*), as *akademi*,

e) Except. 1. All such nouns ending in *i*, which have the accent on the last, as in *fiskeri*, *industri*, *bryggeri*, &c.

2. All nouns ending with *inna* accentuate the last syllable but one, as *värdinna*, hostess; *herdinna*, shepherdess. The same do those in *ska* of foreign origin, *majorska*, mayoress, &c.

3. Verbs ending in *era*, and nouns derived from them, in which the letters *er* are retained, do also accentuate the last syllable but one, as *spatsera*, to take a walk; *plantera*, to plant; *plantering*, plantation, &c.

4. Words beginning with the insep. part. *be* have always the accent on the next syllable to it, as *begynna*, to begin; *besöka*, to

älskarinna, female lover; *adressëra*, to addres;
accentuëring, accentuation, &c.

On the NOUNS.

In stating the genders of the different declensions (see note 5, p. 9) it ought to be observed,
that words, adopted from foreign languages, often
(chiefly in the third declension) make an exception; thus *humör, kapell, concept, lasarett, mirakel,
recept, vin*, &c. are all neuter, although when inflected in plural they terminate in *er*, but the
greatest part of them do belong to the fifth declension: We may say with propriety *ett kapell*,
one chapel, and *många kapell*, many chapels, &c.

Some substantives have a feminine termination
inna, as *Friherre*, Baron; *Friherrinna*, Baroness;
älskare, lover; *älskarinna, Doktor, Doktorinna*.
Others end their feminines with *ska*, as *krögare*,
publican, *krögerska, Major, Majorska*.

A few monosyllabic nouns admit of an emphati-
cal genitive case in the definite state, as *lifsens*,
of the life; *dödsens*, of the death, instead of *lif-
vets, dödens*, which, used with discretion, adds
both energy and beauty to a sentence.

The termination *om*, with which often the da-
tive and ablative cases formerly appeared, as *af*

visit; *besinna*, to remind, &c. Also in words consisting of more
than three syllables, as *besökare*, custom-house officer; *befallan-
de*, commander, &c.

Fadrenom, from the father, is now, with very few exceptions, totally laid aside.

If nouns of the fourth declension admit of the definite article in plural (a few do not), they only add *a* (not *na*) as they terminate with *n;* thus we write *klädena* (of *kläde,* cloth, plur. *kläden*) not *klädenna,* &c.

When nouns of the fifth declension, ending in *are,* are put in the definite state, they are inflected after the second, (to which declension I would have referred them, but for their being the same in singular and pl.). The reason for it is this: They seem to have a double singular, one with and one without the *e* final, of wich the former is used, when the word stands absolute; the latter, when it is joined to another noun, or to a proper name, as *fiskare,* fisherman; *fiskarbåt,* fishing boath; *skräddare,* taylor; *skräddar* Lant, Lant, the taylor. They follow in this the same rule as other uncompounded nouns ending with *e;* thus we say *en Herre,* a Gentleman, but *Herr* Lant, Mr. Lant; *måne,* moon; *månförmörkelse,* eclipse of the moon, and not *Herre Lant, måneförmörkelse.* Now the plural number if inflected after the absolute siugular form *fiskar, skräddar,* must of course (see *obs.* c. page 11) be *fiskrar, skräddrar,* and def. *fiskrarne, skräddrarne,* which last is commonly used in speaking, but the indefinite state in plural is the same as that of the singular, as *en fiskare, många fiskare.* A few indeed such as *hammare,* hammer, and *kammare,* chamber, appeared formerly in the absolute singular form *hammar, kammar,* the indef. plur. of which or *hamrar, kamrar,* is still used, as well as the definite *hamrarne, kamrarne.*

Observe however that among these nouns there are some, that, for the sake of euphony, do not bear to be inflected as we now have stated. Such are, for instance, all those in which there are two *r*'s, as *bärare,* a porter; *körare,* driver, &c. These throw away the *e* final and add *ne* in the def. state in plural, as *bärarne, körarne.* And indeed this mode of inflection is now become the general rule with all these nouns, with the exception of such only, as without the former inflection could not easily be distinguished from other words of a different meaning: Ex. gr. The indef. plural. of *fisk,* fish, is *fiskar,* and the def. of course *fiskarne,* which might be mistaken for the def. pl. of *fiskare,* fisherman, which therefore is *fiskrarne* not *fiskarne.* Formerly these nouns frequently appeared with the full construction, (viz. with the addition of *ne* or *na,* without contraction) to make them definite in plural; but now the termination *ena* seems to be carefully avoided, and when of such words as *klaffare,* backbiter; *dansare,* dancer, &c. the def. state in plur. is required, instead of saying, *klaffarne* (which might be the def. plural of *klaff,* flap) *klaffrarne,* (which sounds rather hard) or *klaffarena; dansarne, dansrarne,* or *dansarena,* we commonly express our thoughts by a different word.

A few nouns have a double termination in plural, when the gender of the word must tell, which is the original, and to what declension they should properly be referred; thus *Bräde (et)* board has in plural *bräden* and *bräder,* and must be referred to the fourth decl. *Man (en)* man, husband, pl. *männer* and *män* to the third. *Tyg (et)* stuff, plur. *tyg* and *tyger* to the fifth. *Mil (en) milar* and *mil* to the second.

Nouns ending with *s* and *x* do not admit of the addition of *s* in the indefinite genitive case, as *is,* ice; *prins,* prince; *vax,* wax: we cannot write *iss, prinss, vaxs;* nor do we ever use an apostrophe, as *is's, prins's, vax's,* for this would indicate the absence of an *e,* and that the gen. was *ises,* &c. it therefore remains the same as in the nominative case, as *en matros skicklighet,* the ability of a sailor, not *matross* or *matros's.* But this genitive case is mostly avoided by construing the word with the particle *af,* as *skönheten af en vers,* the beauty of a verse; *tjockleken af en is,* the thickness of an ice, instead of *en vers skönhet, en is tjocklek.*

When nouns denoting *quantity, number, weight,* and *measure* are placed before other substantives, as descriptive of them, it is seldom wanted in the Swedish language that the particle *af* should be expressed; thus we speak and write correctly:

en hop folk, a crowd of people; *ett dussin hand-skar*, one dozen of gloves; *ett par skor*, a pair of shoes; *ett tjog egg*, a score of eggs; *en mark smör*, a pound of butter; *en tunna tjära*, a barrel of tar; *ett stycke land*, a piece of land; *ett glas vin*, a glass of wine. *Obs.* If the substantive, so described, stands in the definite state, we always find the particle expressed, as *en mark af smöret*, a pound of *the* butter; *ett glas af vinet*, one glass of *the* wine.

A few nouns in the Swedish as well as in the English are used collectively in singular, although they have a plural, as *fånga fisk*, to catch fish; *tre fot lång*, three feet long; *hundratusen man*, hundred thousand men, not *fiskar, fötter, män*, &c.

On *the* ADJECTIVES.

Among the adjectives there are some that form the comparative and superlative degrees by adding only *re* and *st*, not *are* and *ast* (see p. 13), and of these a few change the vowel in the comparisons as *lång*, long, *längre, längst*, not *långre, långst; ung*, young, *yngre, yngst*, not *ungre, ungst*. And others have lost their positive degree, which may be more or less traced in other languages of the same origin; thus for instance *äldre, äldst*, older, oldest, have no positive in the Swedish, but we find it in the English *old* and in several Swedish derivatives, as *ålder*, age; *åldfar*, great grandfather, ancestor; *åldfru*, inspectoress (a title about the court); *åldras*, to grow old, &c.

As the superlative does not, strictly speaking, imply the highest degree, but only a degree beyond the comparative, so we put before it the particle *allra* eller *aller*, very, when we wish to raise it still more in signification, as *det allraminsta*, the very least; *allraödmjukaste*, very humblest, or the humblest of all, &c.

Adjectives, ending with *en*, change that termination into *et* in the neuter gender (see p. 14) except the five following monosyllabics: *Gen*, short (speaking of a road); *klen*, weak; *len*, soft; *ren*, clean; *sen*, late; which there add a *t*, as *gent*, *klent*, *lent*, *rent*, *sent*. And of such adjectives, as end with *t* (which I have stated to remain the same through all the genders) the following nine (also monosyllabics) form an exception: *Fet*, fat; *flat*, flat; *het*, hot; *hvit*, white; *lat*, lazy; *rät*, straight; *slät*, smooth; *söt*, sweet, *våt*, wet. These end the neuter gender with *tt*, as *fett*, *flatt*, *hett*, *hvitt*, *latt*, *rätt*, *slätt*, *sött*, *vått*.

As adjectives, when placed in the definite state, are the same in all genders, except that the vowels *e* and *a* vary in the positive degree (see p. 17), the neuter termination *t* is then always left out, as *det höga hus*, the lofty house, not *det högta hus*, (after the indef. *högt*). The same is observed in the plural number whether the adjective be defin. or indefinite.

Liten neutr. *litet*, little, is irregular in the definite state, as well as in the comparisons: we speak and write *lilla* not *litna*, comp. *mindre*, sup. *minst;* and for the plural number, which *liten* has not, we use a quite different word, viz. *små*, small, which is also irregular in the comparisons, namely, *smärre, smärst*, not *småare, småast. Obs.* The word *små* ought never to be used as a singular; in common conversation we may hear it said *det är smärre*, it is less; *det var det smärsta*, it was the least, but this, I should think, is not correct; custom has however introduced a collective neuter gender of the positive degree, viz. *smått*, which being formed as a singular, is also used as such.

The termination *er* which was formerly added to a number of adjectives, as *glader, goder, feter*, is now never met with in good prose, and but seldom in verse; we now write *glad, god, fet.*

When an adjective is formed from two other adjectives, as *blekgul*, pale yellow, (from *blek* pale and *gul* yellow) *godtrogen*, credulous, from *god* and *trogen*, the latter only is inflected; thus in the genitive case we say *blekguls*, not *bleksguls*, and in the neuter gender *godtroget*, not *godttroget*, &c. NB. The same relates to all other compounded words, except among the pronouns (see page 22).

On the ADJECTIVE *and* SUBSTANTIVE.

As to the place of an adjective, when joined

to a substantive, the Swedish language acknowledges altogether the same rules as the English, as may be seen from the following examples: *En stor dag*, a great day; *långa armar*, long arms; *mannen är lycklig*, the man is happy; *lycklig är den man*, happy is the man; *Alfred den Store*, Alfred the Great; *den Store Alfred*, the Great Alfred; and the same we find when adjectives are explained as participles, ex. gr. *en sak ryslig at se på*, a thing horrid to look on; and I therefore deem all further observations on this subject superfluous.

An adjective, (pronoun or participle, used as an adjective) agrees with its substantive in *gender* and *number*, as *stor man, stort hus, stora hattar; min syster; mitt hus; mine bröder*, my brethren; *en älskad moder*, a beloved mother; *et älskadt barn*, a beloved child; *älskade bröder*, &c. But not so in the cases: In the nominative they are always alike, but if the substantive stands in the genitive case, with its adjective before it, the substantive only is so inflected, as *en stor mans hatt*, the hat of a great man, not *en stors mans hatt*, and definitely, *stora mannens hatt*, not *storas*.

If an adjective be joined to a *proper name*, as expressive of its rank, order, or qualifications, as *Gustaf Adolf den Tappre*, Gustavus Adolphus the Brave, and the context requires that name to be in the genitive case, then the adjective only is so inflected, as *Gustaf den Förstes verk*, the work of Gustavus the First, not *Gustafs den Förstes*, and such adjectives being always preceded by the pronoun, or rather demonstrative particle, *den*, are of course always definite (see page 19).

When an adjective stands absolute, or without its substantive, it may also be inflected in the genitive case, as *en stors*, a great one's, and definitely *den storas*, plur. *de storas*, the great ones. NB. This construction is seldom met with when the adjective is indefinite.

If two or more substantives in the singular number require a verb to be plural, the following adjective is also placed in the plural number, as *handen*, *fingret* och *ringen voro stora*, the hand, the finger, and the ring were great, not *stor;* but if the verb remains in the singular number, the adjective remains there also, as *handen, fingret, och sjelfva ringen var stor*, the hand, the finger, and the ring itself was great, not *stora*, unless we say *voro*.

The right use of the articles being of the greatest moment, I shall endeavour to state distinctly those cases in which substantives and adjectives in this point agree or disagree.

An adjective is placed in the definite state without its substantive being so:

1st. After the *definite pronouns*, as *du vise man*, thou wise man; *din stora stad*, thy great city; not *du vis man*, *din stor stad*, except after *den* and *denne*, which chiefly when signifying *den der* and *den här*, require the substantive also to be definite (see page 19). *Obs*. The word *egen*, neutr. *eget* occurs used both definite and indefinite, after a definite pronoun; we may say *min egna vän* and *min egen vän*, my own friend; *mitt egna bord*, and *mitt eget bord*, my own table, and although the former, or *egna*, is grammatically correct, yet daily use and universal custom has made the other more common, and of course (speaking now of a language) more correct.

2dly. After the interjections, they may be expressed or not, as *O! store konung; ack! lyckliga dag*, or *store konung!* great king; *lyckliga dag!* happy day; except when the indefinite article stands between, as *O! en stor konung, Ack! en lycklig dag*, or when a pronoun follows after the adjective and separates it from its substantive, as *ack! lycklig du konung; ack! säll* den *konung*, *som*, *&c.* O happy the king who, &c.

3dly. When in supplications and addresses it is to be explained in the vocative case, as *Allsmägtige Gud*, Almighty God; *bästa vän*, best friend; not *Allsmägtig Gud, bäst vän*. NB. Whether it be owing to a suppressed interjection or pronoun, that every adjective is definite when used in this case, is here of no use to investigate.

4th. When a noun (pronoun or participle), that belongs to the same sentence, precedes it in the
genitive

genitive case, as *konungens vackra stad*, the king's beautiful city; *en annans goda hatt*, the good hat of another; *den simmandes hvita arm*, the white arm of the swimming (man), not *vacker, god, hvit*. This relates also to the *definite numerals*, when used as adjectives (see note 14 page 22).

An adjective is indefinite although is substantive be definite.

When it is emphatically used as a predicate (and not preceded by *den*), thus, when we say in the English, *great* is the man, or the man is *great*, the Swedish has it, *stor är mannen*, and *mannen är stor;* and this either they stand close to each other, or are separated by one or more intervening words, as *huset, som synes på afstånd, kan vara stort*, the house which is seen at a distance may be great.

Besides in the now mentioned instances an adjective agrees with its substantive in all others *f*).

On *the* PRONOUNS.

The following observations on some of the pronouns may not be thought superfluous.

The personal pronoun *Du*, thou, is much more used in the Swedish language than it is in the

f) Diffident whether I have succeeded in explaining this intricate matter to the satisfaction of my readers, I am the more anxious to see it finally decided by the Swedish Academy; as I have in vain consulted numerous grammarians for a fuller information, and may consequently be mistaken in what I have stated.

English: Man and wife always address themselves by that name; parents use it when speaking to their children, and intimate friends amongst each other. *Obs.* For *Tu, Tin, then* and *thenne,* which mode of spelling occurs in the Bible and the Code of Civil Laws, we now write *Du, Din, den, denne.*

In common conversation we pronounce the words *mig, dig, sig,* as if they were written *mej, dej, sej,* and this is so generally the case, that, in order to speak like others, we are obliged to conform to it. But in oratorial delivery this mode of pronouncing must be carefully avoided.

Before the second person in plural *I* custom has put an *n, (Ni),* which letter, as we know, is the characteristic of that person in all verbs, as *haten, hataden; hafven; varden,* and being used in questions, the final n of the verb seems insensibly to have fallen in with the personal pronoun, as *hafveni* instead of *hafven I;* and thus, *probably,* was *Ni* brought into use instead of *I,* and is now pretty generally admitted, not only in conversation, but even in writing.

Obs. Du (except in the before mentioned cases) and *J* or *Ni* are never used but when speaking to inferiors: We then address a boy or girl *Du,* and a man or woman *Ni.* When we write or speak to superiors, or such as we owe respect, or wish to be polite to, we use the words *Herre,* Sir; *Fru,*

Madam; *Fröken, Mamsell, Jungfru g*), Miss, &c.
which are then (except those that end with *n* as
Baron, and also the word *Mamsell*) put in the
definite state, as *vill Herren h*) *gå?* do you wish
to go, Sir? *har Frun sett det?* have you seen it,
Madam? but *vill Fröken gå?* har *Mamsell sett det?*
In the plural number all these complimentary words
and titles are put in the definite state, as *ha Ba-
ronerna varit der?* have you been there, Barons?
huru må Damerna? (of *Dam,* lady) how do you
do, ladies? This relates also to the family names *Fader, Moder, Broder* and *Syster,* as *ha Systrarna sett
det?* have you seen it, Sisters? but in singular these
must be indefinite, as *har syster,* (not *systren*) *sett
det?* If besides the words *Herre* and *Fru* the title
of the person also is mentioned (which in politer
addresses always is observed) then these words remain in the indefinite state, but the title is placed in
the definite, as *vill Fru Majorskan komma?* not
Frun, and in this case the final *e* of the word
Herre, is, as I have before stated *), always left
out, as *vill Herr Majoren komma? Herr Doktorn
var ej hemma,* you were not at home, Doctor, &c.

---

g) We address a Nobleman's daughter, *Fröken;* a Gentleman's
daughter, *Mamsell;* and those of the third class, *Jungfru,* which
signifies *virgin* or *maid.*

h) The word *Herre* is (in the definite state) pronounced *Herrn,* and
even frequently written so.

*) See page 57, where I speak of the nouns ending with *are.*

Honom (of *han*), *henne* (of *hon*) and *det* suffer a strange contraction in speaking: Instead of saying *honom* they only add an *n* to the preceding word, as *har du sett'n* for *har du sett honom?* and instead of *henne* and *det*, they add in the same manner *na* and *t*, as *se'na* for *se henne*, *se på't* for *se på det;* but these abreviations, though too commonly used in familiar conversation, are far from being elegant, and ought to be avoided as much as possible.

Vårs is an obsolete genitive sing. of *Vår*, and occurs only in the Scriptures. *Eders*, the gen. sing. of *Eder* is used before titles, as *Eders Nåd*, your Grace; *Eders Höghet*, your Highness; *Eders Kungliga Majestät*, your Royal Majesty. *Obs.* As *J* or *Ni* can never be used, but when they may be explained in the nominative or rather vocative case, the word *Eder* supplies the other cases, and is then always contracted into *Er:* We cannot say, *Jag gaf det åt Ni, Jag har sett J, Jag hade det från Ni*, but *Jag gaf det åt Er*, I gave it to you; *Jag har sett Er*, I have seen you; *Jag hade det från Er*, I had it from you. The same contraction we find even when *eder* is used as an adjective, as *er son är stor*, your son is great; and in the neuter gender, *är det ert barn?* is it your child? Whether it were right to use *eder* when it stands absolute or separated from its substantive, as *det är edert*, it is yours; *Boken är eder*, the book is yours, and *er* when it is joined to a substantive, as *det är er son*, it is your son, I will not take upon myself to determine. Certain it is, that this distinction is not attended to.

Of *sin* neutr. *sitt*, I have spoken already (see p. 20) Here I will only add, that although this pronoun is used as an adjective, it never (as also may be seen from the English words set against it) occurs in the nominative case. I make this observation as I have found foreigners frequently mistake this point. We cannot say, *Han och sin Far* (contr. for *Fader*) *komma; han sade at sin mor* (contr. for *moder*) *är hemma; de och sina vänner äro här;* but *Han och hans Far komma; Han sade at hans mor är hemma; De och deras vänner äro här,* they and their friends are here; or in the ablative case, *Han kom med sin far; de äro här med sina vänner;* and in the accusative, *Han sade sin moder vara hemma,* (*matrem domi esse*). Observe too that *sin* always refers to the *active substantive,* or, to speak with the acute Mr. Harris *i*), the *energizer* of the sentence; thus, *han var i sitt hus,* he was in his house, is correct; but we cannot say, *Jag var hos honom i sitt hus,* it must be *i hans hus,* for here *Jag* is the energizer, but in the former instance *han.*

The indefinite pronoun *någon,* any, is in the neuter gender *något,* and in plural *någre* or *några.* gen. *någras. Ingen,* no or none, neutr. *intet,* plur.

i) See his Hermes, B. i. C. ix.

inga. NB. *Intet* is in common conversation frequently used for *ej* or *icke*, as *jag har det intet (ej)*, I have it not; but we cannot with propriety use it so in writing.

The demonstrative pronoun *den*, that, is sometimes used as a relative (for *som* or *hvilken*), when the preceding noun is indefinite; we may say: *En väg, den jag kan gå*, a road that I can go, but not (it seems) with propriety, *vägen den jag kan gå;* for *vägen*, being definite already (and we may resolve it into *den väg*) needs no further definition, and we therefore write, *vägen, som jag kan gå.*

Hvilken (see p. 22) when used either in questions or as a relative, must agree in gender and number with the noun to which it refers, as *hvilken (man) såg du? hvilket (band) vill du se?* and in the genitive case *hvilkens (hvilken mans) är det? hvilkets (hvilket sällskaps) är det?* to what company does it belong? *Han söker den lön, hvilken han vet sig förtjena*, he seeks the reward which he is conscious he deserves; *han fruktar för hafvet, hvilket han tror vara farligt*, he fears the sea, which he believes to be dangerous.

The pronoun *hvad*, what, is often (chiefly in questions) followed by the particle *för*, as *hväd för fisk?* what kind of fish? *hvad för en man?* what man? But I have not observed this to be admitted in classical writings.

In page 18 I have called *en* a pronoun, as it

sometimes occurs in a signification, which is neither that of the article, nor of the numeral *en*, as *en (och annan)* one (and another) and definitely *den ene*, the one, and as such it occurs also in the compounded pronouns *enhvar, hvarochen*, &c.

On the VERBS.

The Verbs have been examined already in the paradigmatical part of this work as to their different kinds and inflections; here I shall only add a few observations on them, which I look upon as necessary to be known by a beginner.

When we do not want to determine any certain person or persons of a verb, we use the pronoun *man*, which on that account, (and not that it is used before impersonal verbs, which it never can be), I have called impersonal, though it, strictly speaking, comprehends all the persons, as *man kan lätt se det*, one can (or may) easily see it; *man har sagt mig det*, I am told so, &c.

The Auxiliary verbs receive often a positive signification, by the stress laid on them in pronunciation; Thus, for instance, *Jag kan gå, jag skall blifva*, may be explained three different ways: If we *first* lay the stress on *kan* and *skall*, it signifies that it is *in my power (jag kan)* to go, and that I *absolutely must (jag skall)* be; and if we let it rest on *gå* and *blifva*, the meaning depends then on the signification of those verbs; *lastly*, we may lay all the stress on *Jag*, if we wish to express *who* it is, that *kan gå* and *skall blifva;* but this, being the same in all languages, is easily understood by itself; I mention it merely to show the necessity of attending to the most probable meaning of the sentence, which often may have as many different turns almost, as there are words in it; the following well known question will prove this: *Förråder du menniskones *) Son med kyssande?* betrayest thou the Son of man with a kiss?

It must further be observed of the auxiliary verbs, that some of them often appear by themselves, and have then also a positive sense; thus *hafva* signifies to possess, *blifva* to remain, *kunna* to know, &c. as *Jag kan min lexa,* I know my lesson; *Jag blifver i London,* I remain in London; *han har stora egendomar,* he possesses large estates, &c. but this practice must teach.

As *at få,* to get, to receive, is often used as an auxiliary verb in the Swedish, I think it proper to observe that it is translated into English different ways, as the meaning of the sentence may require; thus *Jag får der höra talas om honom* we translate, I *will* there hear him be spoken of; *Jag får gå dit om jag vill,* I *may* go there if I like; *Jag fick icke göra det,* I *was not permitted* to do it; *Jag fick ej tid,* I *had* no time; *du får lof at*

---

*) *Menniskones* is a biblical genitive case in the definite state for *menniskans.*

göra det, it *is your right* to do it; *de fingo sina penningar*, they *received* their money, &c.

When a whole sentence, or an infinitive mode, is the subject of a verb, it is always put in the singular number and third person, as *deras för-nöjda ansigten var det som fägnade mig*, (litterally) their happy countenances was it that pleased me; *at älska sitt fädernesland är en angenäm pligt*, to love one's country is a joyful duty; for these phrases may be resolved thus: *det var deras förnöjda ansigten som fägnade mig*, *det är en an-genäm pligt at älska sitt fädernesland*, whereby *det* becomes the nominative in the sentence.

The active verbs in the Swedish express their passives in the following manners: *Jag älskas, Jag är älskad*, and *jag blifver* or *varder älskad*, of which the *first*, or *jag älskas*, indicates what is done, or exists in the present moment; the *second*, or *jag är älskad*, means what has already existed some time and still exists, and the *third*, jag *blifver* or *varder älskad*, has reference to a time, wich suc-ceeds the present; thus if I say *Jag hatas, jag värmes*, it meens that I am now in the actual state of being hated or warmed; *Jag är hatad, jag är värmd* implies, that I have been so for some time, and still continue so, and *jag varder hatad, jag blifver värmd*, that I am to be so. But to explain it by another example, let us take the verb *sticka*, to sting, to stab: If we want to express that two

persons are now in the aet of being stung, we
say, *de stickas*, if they are stung already: *de äro
stuckne*, and if they are to be stung: *de blifva
stuckne*. And in the imperfect tense: *Jag älskades*,
means I was loved: *Jag var älskad*, I was and had
been loved, and *jag vardt* or *blef älskad*, I became loved (not having been so before).

For the sake of perspicuity the compounded
passive forms are sometimes used instead of the
simple. I will show the necessity of this by an
example: The passive of the verb *at slå*, to beat,
is *jag slås*, imp. *jag slogs*, but there is also a demi-
passive or *deponent* verb *at slåss*, to fight, which
has the imperfect tense the same as the other, or
jag slogs. Now if I was to say *Ryssarne slogos*,
it might either signify that the Russians fought,
or that the Russians were defeated, we therefore
in the latter case use *varda* or *blifva*, as *Ryssarne
slogos tappert vid Svensksund, men blefvo slagne*,
the Russians fought bravely at *Svensksund*, but
were defeated.

Obs. All the difference I can trace between
varda and *blifva* is, that *varda* seems to be used
when a greater emphasy is required, and that it
implies a stronger assertion than *blifva*. Besides
it never occurs in a positive sense as *blifva* does,
but always as an auxiliary verb.

Of the impersonal verbs some appear in an
active and others in a passive form, as *det regnar*,

it rains; *det dagas*, it begins to dawn; of the verbs *at regna*, to rain; and *at dagas*, to dawn. *Obs.* Verbs of all kinds may be used as impersonal in the Swedish, in the same manner as they are in the English, as *der gick et rygte*, there was a rumour; *det syntes så*, it appeared so; *de säga mycket som icke är sant*, they say much that is not true; *man kunde ej komma in*, one could not get in, &c.

Neuter verbs, or such as have the energizer and the passive subject united in the same person, are easily distinguished from actives by their not requiring an accusative, as *Jag faller*, I fall; *Jag sofver*, I sleep, &c.

A few verbs appeared formerly with a double imperative mode; thus we find *gack* and *gå*, of the verb *at gå*; *statt* and *stå*, of *at stå*, to stand; but the former of these (*gack, statt*) are now totally laid aside, and occur only in the Scriptures and writings of an antique date.

As Imperatives not only imply a command, but also frequently a wish, or exhortation, &c. as *bevara, Gud! vår kung*, God save our king; *strid, Hjelte! strid*, fight, Hero! fight, we use the sign of the future tense when we wish to enforce a command, as *du skall arbeta*, thou shalt work; *J skolen göra det*, you shall (or must) do it.

The sign of the infinitive mode (*at*) is often left out in the Swedish, where in the English it must be expressed; thus we write correctly *Jag bör göra det*, I ought *to* do it; *Jag ser läsa*, I see *to* read, &c.

The form of the participles may be learnt from the paradigms; here I will only, the better to distinguish them to beginners, observe, that the present participles, both active and passive, occur after the auxiliary verbs *vara*, *varda*, and *blifva*, and the preterite participles after *hafva*, as *jag är, jag varder, jag blifver hatande*, and *hatad*, I am, I will be hating and hated, but *jag hafver hatat*, I have hated, *jag hafver hatats*, I have been hated; *det är hatadt, skrifvet*, it is hated, written, *det har hatat, skrifvit*, it has hated, written; *det är gjordt*, it is done; *jag har gjort det*, I have done it, &c.

The present active participle occurs often in the English, where the Swedish does not admit of it: We can neither begin a sentence with it, nor use it immediately after another verb; thus if we would translate, 'having no money to lay out,' and 'I cannot help admiring him,' we could not say, *hafvande inga penningar at lägga ut; jag kan ej underlåta beundrande honom;* but must in the former case begin the sentence with a particle, and in the latter, place the verb in the infinitive mode, as *såsom jag har inga penningar at lägga ut; Jag kan ej underlåta at beundra honom.* No more can we use it after any of the particles, as is often the case in the English. The following expressions should thus be rendered into Swedish: 'After having done that,

I came home,' *sedan jag hade gjort det, kom jag hem;* 'I am prevented from doing it,' *jag är hindrad från at göra det;* 'I saw it whilst I was sitting there,' *jag såg det medan jag satt der,* &c. This participle occurs however sometimes with the preposition *i* (in) before it; as *han öfvergår mig i talande,* he excels me in speaking; but even here I think it more correct to use the infinitive mode, although it might be alledged, that the verb, so used, is no longer a participle but a *noun.*

Obs. This participle is always used, when it could not be exchanged for the infinitive mode without altering the meaning of the sentence, as *han stod der talande,* he stood there speaking; *han stod der at tala* would be, he stood there in order to speak. Besides it implies a longer continuation of the present, and is more descriptive than the infinitive mode: *Jag hörde honom talande,* I heard him speaking, says more than, *Jag hörde honom tala;* but in this case it is a verbal adjective, and may, as such, even begin a sentence, as *talande stod han der,* &c.

This participle is further inflected with an *s* in the genitive case, as *en talandes, en älskandes,* which must not be confounded with the gerundial forms (see note 20, p. 32). The difference between the active gerund and the participle may be learnt from the following example: *Han mötte mig ridandes,* he met me riding (eqvitando mihi obviam venit): here *ridandes* is the gerund and refers to *han;* but if we say, *han mötte mig ridande,* he met me riding (eqvitanti mihi obviam venit), then *ridande* is the participle and refers to *mig k*).

Should the preposition *til* (to), which is the sign of the passive gerund not add an *s* to the participle when it stands before it, it remains active, and is best translated with the infinitive mode, as *jag nämner det til bevisande af hans heder,* I mention it *to prove* his honour.

The auxiliary verb *hafva* is often suppressed (even in writing) when no confusion in the sentence arises from it, which in the English in similar cases would be unavoidable, as *om han hatat mig, så skulle jag glömt det,* for *om han hade hatat mig så skulle jag hafva glömt det,* if he (had) hated me, I should (have) forgot it; *om jag endast haft tid,* for *om jag endast hade haft tid,* if I only (had) had time, &c. Besides *hafva* is contracted into *ha,* and *hafver* into *har,* which is also admitted both in speaking and writing.

In the present tense of the verb *vara* the contraction (in speaking) is still greater, for here often

k) It is on the authority of Mr. SAHLSTEDT (see his Grammar, p. 48) that I have stated this difference between *ridandes* and *ridande.* Undoubtedly the language would gain by it, if what this able grammarian observes on the subject, is consistent with its present genius. For my part I am dubious on that head; but till it is decided by better judges, I bow with reverence to the statements of a man, who in so many other instances has been my teacher.

one letter only is retained, as *jag ä glad at de ä här* for *jag är glad at de äro här;* and in the imperfect tense we will hear *va* used for all the persons, as *Jag, du, han va glad at vi, J, de va der*, I, &c. was glad, that we, &c. were there. In the same manner we say *blir* for *blifver,* (which also appears in writing); *ska* for *skall; skull* for *skulle,* &c.

Vill and *kan* are also in common conversation not inflected, as *vill ni gå* for *viljen J gå? kan ni göra det* for *kunnen J göra det?* can you do it?

Obs. Of *måste*, must, we form a preterite act. participle *måst*, as *han har måst göra det*, he has been obliged to do it.

The other verbs suffer more or less contraction in speaking. In general we may observe of them, that the first person (sing. and plur.) is retained through all the others without inflection. Observe that in the first conjugation, the imperfect tense (the characteristic of which is to be trisyllabical) leaves out the termination *de;* thus they will say *han hata mig*, instead of *han hatade mig*, &c.

Verbs of the second conjugation, as also irregular verbs, ending with *ara, ära,* and *öra,* do generally become monosyllabic in the singular number of the present tense; thus instead of *lärer, körer,* from the verbs *lära,* to learn; *köra,* to drive, &c. we use *lär, kör.*

The first person in plural of all verbs in the Swedish language were formerly ended with *e,* as *vi hafve, vi hate, vi höre,* &c. which termination, though it still may be met with, begins more and more to be laid aside in writing, as it has long been in speaking.

In order the better to distinguish the neuter gender of the present passive participle from the preterite active in the irregular verbs, I have in the paradigms and examples retained the old mode of terminating the former with *et* (in which form it yet frequently appears) as *funnet, skrifvet, taget,* and the latter with it, *funnit, skrifvit, tagit;* but this distinction is now laid aside, since the termination *it* became prevalent in speaking: We now write *du har funnit* and *det är funnit* l).

On the PARTICLES.

I shall now close my observations with a few remarks on the particles, some of which have no correspondents in the English, and may therefore appear either superfluous or intricate to a beginner.

Så is the sign of the *apodosis* or subsequent meaning of the sentence, as *om jag kan* så *vill jag,* if I can I will, and always places the nominative after its verb, *när han kom dit* så *sade mannen til honom,* not så *mannen sade,* when he came

there

---

l) Observe here also that the article *et* (except when added to a noun as in *bord*et, the table) is of late, as well as the numeral and pronoun *ett*, written with *tt,* as *ett bord,* a table.

here the man said to him. *Obs. Så* is often suppressed, but the construction is still the same, as
när jag kom, sade han, not *han sade.*

The affirmative particle *sannnerligen,* indeed,
verily, is negative when the following nominative
stands before its verb, as *sannerligen jag kan,* indeed I cannot, but affirmative if *vice versa,* as *san-*
nerligen kan jag, indeed I can; and if a negative
particle is added to the sentence, it does not alter
this rule, but only strengthens the assertion, as
sannerligen jag kan icke, indeed I cannot, *sanner-*
ligen kag jag icke, indeed I can. The place of
the nominative and its verb should therefore be
particularly attended to, as the meaning of the
whole sentence often depends on it.

Der, there, and *här,* here, signify the being in a
place, *dit* and *hit,* thither and hither, the going to,
and coming from a place *m)*, as *han är här,* he is
here; *kom hit,* come hither; *han stod der,* he stood
here; *han gick dit,* he went thither. *Obs.* this
distinction is strictly attended to in the Swedish.

At, which is the note of the infinitive mode, signifies also the same as *that,* as *de hoppas at han*
vill komma, they hope *that* he will come. *Obs.* The

m) Observe the same of *inne,* within, and *in,* in; as *han är inne,*
he is within, *kom in,* come in.

6

pronoun *det* is sometimes used instead of *at;* thus they will say; *de hoppas* det *han vill komma,* &c.

The interrogative particle *ju,* having no correspondent in the English, is there best expressed by giving the meaning the turn of an affirmative question, as *jag kan* ju *icke det?* is not that impossible for me? *Han är* ju *stor?* is he not great? But when it precedes an adjective in the comparative degree, it answers to *the,* as ju *mer desto bättre,* the more the better.

Väl is another interrogative particle without a correspondent, and must be rendered by *indeed, I suppose, I hope,* &c. as the meaning of the sentence may require, as *det kunde du* väl, that you could indeed; *han är* väl *icke hemma?* he is not at home, I suppose? *han är* väl *här?* he is here I hope? *Obs. Väl* signifies also *well,* and for the interjection *well!* the Swedish language has *nå väl! välan!*

Nog, enough, must also sometimes be rendered with *indeed,* as *han vill* nog *göra det, om du ber honom,* he will *indeed* (or certainly) do it, if you tell him.

The interrogative particle *månne* is used in plain questions, as *månne det är sant?* do you think it is true? *månne han kommer?* is it expected that he will come? &c.

Between *ja* and *jo,* which are both translated with *yes,* this difference is to be observed, that *jo* is used after questions in which there is a negative particle, as *var han* ej *der?* was he not there? *jo;* and *ja* after such in which there is none, as *kom han dit?* did he come thither? *ja. Obs. Jo* is in common conversation frequently used as a mere affirmative interjection, as *hvad skall jag nu göra?* what must I now do? *jo! du skall skrifva,* you must write.

Qvar is variously translated, as may be seen from the following examples: *är något qvar?* is any thing left? *han satt qvar,* he kept sitting; *är hon ännu qvar?* is she still here? *Doktorn blef qvar,* the Doctor remained, &c.

The inseparable particles, such as *be, för, miss, o, an,* &c. in b*eströ,* to bestrew; *för*dom, prejudice; miss*förstånd,* misunderstanding; o*lycklig,* unhappy; an*taga,* to take upon, to accept, are easily learnt by practice.

The following words, which might be called *demi-adverbs,* are formed by joining a particle to a noun either in the nominative or genitive case. They are all such as constantly occur: *i morgon,* to morrow; *i öfvermorgon,* the day after tomorrow; *om bord,* on board; *om söndag, om måndag, &c.* next sunday, next monday, &c. *I söndags, i måndags, &c.* last sunday, last monday, &c. *I fjol,* last year; *åt året* or *åt åres,* next year; *i vår,* next spring; *i våras,* last spring; *i sommar,* next summer; *i höst,* next autumn; *i höstas,* last autumn;

i vinter, next winter; *i vintras*, last winter; *til han is*, at hand; *til handa*, to hand; *efter hand*, little by little; *öfver hufvud*, upon an average; *intil sjös*, at sea; *utom lands*, abroad; *inom lands*, within one's country, &c.

But attention in reading a language is the best teacher of grammar, and the few rules I have now laid down will assist in finding the rest.

A PRAXIS.

~~~~~~~~

Containing some scattered Pieces in Prose and Poetry, from which the connexion of the different parts of speech, and the construction of a sentence, will easily be inferred. They are borrowed from classical writers, and selected for this work on account of their syntactical perspicuity.

SORGENS SON *)

Vid hafvet på ensliga stranden
　　Satt Sorgen, från himmelen skild,
Och formade, tankfull, med handen
　　Af leret en menniskobild 1).

Zevs kom. Hvad är det? hörs han fråga.
　　»O, Gud! blott en skapnad af ler;
Men visa din guda-förmåga,
　　Gif lif åt den bild som du ser.« 2)

*) THE SON OF SORROW.

A litteral translation.

1) Near the sea on the lonely shore sat Sorrow, excluded from heaven, and formed thoughtful with her (the) hand a human image of clay.

2) Jove came. What is this? he is heard to ask. O God! only a shape of clay, but show Thy divine power, give it spirit and life (give life to the image, which Thou beholdest).

Han lefve; likväl jag förklarar:
  Min är han i kraft af mitt lån.
» Nej, « (utbrister Sorgen och svarar),
  » Nej, låt mig behålla min son. 3)

» Af mig är han tilskapad vorden. «
  Ja; men han har lifvet af mig.
Som Jofur det sade, kom Jorden,
  Såg bilden och yttrade sig: 4)

» Från mig, från mitt sköt är han röfvad,
  » Jag återbegär hvad jag mist. «
Er rätt, sade Zevs, skall bli pröfvad,
  Saturnus skall slita vår tvist. 5)

Han dömde: » Sig ingen beklage!
  » Til alla gemensamt han hör.
» Du Zevs! som gaf lifvet, det tage
  » Med anden igen när han dör. 6)

3) May he live, but now he is mine (yet I declare mine he is) in
   consequence of my loan. No, exclaims Sorrow and answers, no,
   let me retain my son.

4) I was the person that made him (of me he has been shaped). Yes,
   but I gave him life. As Jove said this, Earth came, saw the Figure
   and spoke (uttered herself):

5) From me, from my bosom he is torn (robbed), and I reclaim
   what I have lost. Your right answered Jove shall be examined:
   Saturn shall decide between us (determine our dispute).

6) He gave this sentence (he judged): May no one complain! This
   image (he) belongs to you all. Thou Jove! who gave him life,
   take it again with his soul, when he dies.

» Du Jord! til din egendom göre
  » Hans ben. Göm dem åter i frid.
» Dig Sorg! Dig sin mor han tilhöre
  » Sin hela besvärliga tid. 7)

» Från dig skall, så länge han andas,
  » Han aldrig bli skild någon dag.
» Din suck med hans anda skall blandas;
  » Din blick med hans anletes drag. « 8)

Så Allmagtens utslag blef gifvet,
  Och menskan, i kraft af Dess bud,
Blef tilhörig Sorgen i lifvet;
  I döden — Jorden och Gud. 9)

Om Ledsnaden 1).

Ledsnaden, säger man, är vår farligaste fiende 2).
Det tror jag nog. Hon är värre än döden och för-
gängelsen 3). Hon beröfvar 4) oss känslan af lif-
vets behag 5), utan at, som dessa, beröfva oss sak-

---

7) Thou Earth! make to thy possession his bones. Hide them again
in peace. To thee, Sorrow! to thee, his mother, he is to belong
his whole troublesome time.

8) From thee he shall, as long as he breathes, never be separated
any day. Thy sigh shall be mixed with his breath, thy look with
the features of his face.

9). So the decree of the Almighty was given, and man, in consequence of that (his command), is to belong (became belonging) to
Sorrow for life; in death — to Earth and to God.

1. Wearisomeness. 2. Most dangerous enemy. 3. Destruction. 4. To
deprive. 5. Sense of the pleasures of life.

naden deraf. Man har kallat henne en förminsk-
ning 6) af vår varelse. Denna metafysiska jargon
vill säga i förnuftigt språk 7), at hon beröfvar oss
de angenäma känslor 8), som göra vår sällhet. Man
saknar 9) hvad man vill eller kunde njuta 10).
En bokvurm leds 11) efter sina böcker, en älskare
efter sin skönas 12) umgänge. En resande främling 13) efter stillheten af sin lugnare hembygd 14).

Helvetius påstår 15), at det är ledsnaden som
vi hafve at tacka för en stor del af vår varelses
fullkomlighet. Det vill säga 16): (ty man måste ofta
förklara 17) hvad en filosof vill säga) det vill då
säga, til deras uplysning 18), som äro det mindre
än jag, at ledsnaden, som satt oss i behof af nya
sysslor och nöjen 19), fört 20) oss til upfinning
af dessa konster och vetenskaper 21), som förädla
och förljufva 22) sammanlefnaden 23). I det fallet
24) är hon en plågo-ande 25), som födt 26) englar.

Man skulle kunna säga, om man ville vara fin
27), at Helvetius har orätt 28). Det är icke ledsnaden, det är snarare behaget af arbete, som alstrat
dessa vetenskaper och dessa konster. Ledsnaden
har aldrig 29) frambragt något annat än oduglighet

6. Diminution. 7. Language. 8. Pleasing sensations. 9 To miss.
10. To enjoy. 11. To grow sad. 12. Mistress. 13. Travelling stranger.
14. More peaceful home. 15. To maintain. 16. That is to say.
17. To explain. 18. Information. 19. In want of new occupations
and pleasures 20. To lead. 21. Arts an sciences. 22. To charm
23. Society. 24. In that case. 25. A fury. 26. To bring forth. 27.
Subtil. 28. *At ha orätt*, to be in the wrong. 29. To breed, to pro-

och afsmak 30). Det är hennes motsatt*a* god*a* ande 51), arbetsnöje*t* 32), som föder nytta och sällhet 33). Ledsnade*n* var alltid ofruktsam 34). De
Gamle hafva haft rätt 35) at föreställa 36) henne
lam, med hängande hufvud 37), blekt ansigte 38)
och ryckningar af vämjelse 39) vid alla ämnen 41).

Kanske måste man dock göra en åtskillnad 41).
Det gifves en fullkomlig 42) ledsnad, och en ledsnad för ögonblicke*t* 43). Denna sednare 44) är
ej annat än tomhet 45) på känslor, en saknad af
nöje*t*, som drifver oss at söka det: den förr*a* 46)
är en afsmak för alla, och en sjukdom 47). Dessa
begge slag 48) skiljas åt som hunger och äckel
49); *).

duce. 30. Futility and disgust. 31. Good Genius. 32 Love of labour. 33. Which brings benefit and happiness. 34. Unfruitful. 35.
The Ancients have been in the right. 36. To represent. 37. Head.
38. Pale countenance. 59 Shrugs of displeasure (loathing). 40. At
all subjects. 41. Distinction. 42. Complete, standing. 43. Moment.
44 Latter. 45. Vacancy, want. 46. The former. 47. Disease. 48.
These two kinds. 49. Loathing

*) The reader will find the continuation of this piece among the
collected works of *C. G. Leopold*, T. iii. p. 458.

DEN ALLMÄNNA BÖNEN.

Öfversatt från Engelskan.

O Fader! hvad Du månde heta,
Jehovah, Jofur, eller Gud:
De vise Dina stadgar veta,
De vilde känna Dina bud.

Du varelsernas första källa,
Som ingen dödlig än förstod,
Må evigt denna sanning gälla,
At jag är blind, och Du är god!

Du gaf förmögenhet at skilja
I detta mörker ondt från godt;
Och lemnade åt menskans vilja
Den frihet ej naturen fått.

Låt allt, som strider mot Din ära,
Låt allt, hvaraf den blir förökt,
Långt mer än helvetet förfära,
Långt mer än himlen blifva sökt!

Låt mig i tacksamt minne sluta
Allt godt, som Du mig lemnat har:
Ty menskor lyda, då de njuta,
Gud är betald, när menskan tar.

Låt mig ej all Din godhet skränka
Inom den krets, som jag bebor:
Jag tusen verldars Gud Dig tror,
Då tusen verldar kring mig blänka.

Låt mig ej tro Du skulle ge
Åt mig den magt at åskan tända,

THE UNIVERSAL PRAYER,

Translated by Mr. N. L. SJÖBERG.

FATHER of All! in ev'ry age,
  In ev'ry clime ador'd,
By saint, by savage, and by sage,
  Jehovah, Jove, or Lord?

Thou Great First Cause, least understood,
  Who all my sense confin'd
To know but this, that Thou art good,
  And that myself am blind;

Yet gave me, in this dark estate,
  To see the good from ill;
And binding nature fast in fate,
  Left free the human will.

What conscience dictates to be done,
  Or warns me not to do,
This, teach me more than hell to shun,
  That, more than heav'n pursue.

What blessings Thy free bounty gives,
  Let me not cast away;
For God is paid when man receives:
  T' enjoy is to obey.

Yet not to earth's contracted span,
  Thy goodness let me bound.
Or think Thee Lord alone of man,
  When thousand worlds are round.

Let not this weak, unknowing hand
  Presume Thy bolts to throw,

Och hämnden kring om jorden sända
Til den jag tror Din fiende.

Om jag gör rätt, o låt mig vinna
Mer styrka på den väg jag far!
Om jag går villse, låt mig finna
Den stråten jag förlorat har!

Må Du mig aldrig se förmäten,
Om någon nåd Du mig vill ge!
Må Du mig aldrig missnöjd se,
Om någon gång jag blir förgäten!

Hvad andra brutit må bli glömdt!
Hvad andra lida må jag ömma!
Må Du en gång om mig så dömma,
Som jag om alla andra dömt!

Fast jag är svag, är det min styrka
At ha min anda ifrån Dig:
I dag, ehvad som händer mig,
Må jag Dig värdigt kunna dyrka?

Bröd, helsa, frid, den lotten blif,
Som Du i dag må mig beskära!
Allt annat neka, eller gif,
Allt som det sämjes med Din ära.

Åt Dig, Du högsta varelse,
Som rymden til Ditt tempel spände,
Och jorden satt til altare,
Må alla röster låfsång ge!
Må alla rökverk blifva tände!

And deal damnation round the land,
　　On each I judge Thy foe.

If I am right, Thy grace impart,
　　Still in the right to stay:
If I am wrong, oh! teach my heart
　　To find that better way.

Save me alike from foolish pride,
　　Or impious discontent,
At aught Thy wisdom has deny'd,
　　Or aught Thy goodness lent.

Teach me to feel another's woe,
　　To hide the fault I see;
That mercy I to others show,
　　That mercy shew to me.

Mean tho' I am, not wholly so,
　　Since quick'ned by Thy breath:
O lead me wheresoe'er I go,
　　Thro' this day's life or death.

This day, be bread and peace my lot:
　　All else beneath the sun,
Thou know's if best bestow'd or not,
　　And let Thy will be done.

To Thee, whose temple is all space,
　　Whose altar, earth, sea, skies,
One chorus let all Beings raise!
　　All nature's incense rise!

————

*Om främmande ord i Svenska Språk*et 1).

Ifrån äldsta tider 2) hade Svenska språk*et* blifvi upblandadt med främmande ord. Troligen 3) har någon sammanblandning skett 4) emellan det språk Asarne hitförde 5), och det som talades af land*ets* äldsta inbyggare 6); men dess beskaffenhet 7) och följder kunna af oss svårligen 8) kännas 9) och bestämmas 10). Språk*et* tog sedermera efter hand sin form och sitt lynne 11). Behof och tilfällig-heter 12) hafva tid efter annan upfyllt det med lån ifrån åtskilliga tungomål 13). Förnämligast hafva dock de främmande ord vi äga, kommit ifrån dessa fem språk: Latin*en*, Engelska*n*, Dan-ska*n*, Tyska*n* 14) och Franska*n*, &c. &c.

Då Christendom*en* infördes, fingo vi helt visst ur Engelska*n* flera 15) ord. Begge språk*ens* ge-mensamm*a* ursprung 16), som vid denna epok vi-sade 17) sig i större likhet än nu för tid*en*, gjorde dock införlifvand*et* 18) af dessa ord lätt, och utan betydlig 19) verkan på uttal och skrifssätt 20); och skulle någon sådan hafva inträffat 21), förlo-

1. On foreign words in the Swedish language, (extracted from the preface to the Transactions of the Sw. Academy, p. 31). 2. Re-motest times. 3. Probably. 4. *At ske*, to happen, to take place. . *At hitföra*, to bring hither. 6. Inhabitants. 7 Nature. 8 Hardly. 9. To know. 10. To determine. 11. Genius, turn. 12. Chance, oc-currence. 13. Different languages. 14. The German. 15. Several. 16. Common origin. 17. To show. 18. Incorporation, naturalization. 19. Material. 20. Pronunciation and orthography. 21. To occur,

rar den sig i en ålderdom, der undersökning*en*
22) blir svår 23), om icke omöjlig 24).

to arrive, to take place. 22. Investigation, scrutiny. 23. Difficult.
24. Impossible.

~~~~~~

SAMTAL.	DIALOGUES.
God morgon. God dag.	Good morning. Good day.
God afton. Farväl.	Good evening. Farewell.
Hur mår Herrn?	How do you do, Sir?
Hur står det til?	How are you?
Hur har Herrn mått?	How have you been?
Bra, Gud vare låf!	Well, God be thanked!
Rätt bra, jag tackar.	Very well, I thank you.
Jag mår rätt väl nu; men jag har varit illa sjuk.	I am very well now; but I have been very ill.
Jag beklagar det mycket; men jag är glad at se Herrn åter frisk.	I am very sorry for it; but I am glad to see you well again.
Ärnar Herrn resa längre i afton?	Do you intend to travel farther this evening?
Nej, jag blir qvar här i natt.	No, I remain here to night.
Jag ärnar hvila här öfver natten.	I intend to sleep here to night.
Blir Herrn ock qvar?	Do you stay likewise, Sir?
Jag reser hela natten.	I shall travel all night.
Jag (tycker om) at resa om natten;	I (like) to travel by night;
Ty det är svalare då.	Because it is cooler then.

Man möter ej så mycket folk.	One does not meet so much people.
Hvart ärnar Herrn resa?	Whither do you intend to travel, Sir?
Tänker Herrn resa långt?	Do you think to travel far?
Jag reser til Harwich, och derifrån far jag til Sverige.	I am travelling to Harwich, and from thence I shall sail for Sweden.
Vet Herrn när Paketen går?	Do you know, Sir, when the packet goes?
Jag går med et skepp.	I go in a ship.
Paketen går i morgon, om vinden är god.	The packet goes to morrow, if the wind is fair.
Är Herrn säker på det?	Are you sure of that, Sir?
Vet Herrn det visst?	Do you know it for certain, Sir?
Ja, det är ganska säkert.	Yes, it is very certain.
Det är osäkert.	It is uncertain.
Jag är viss på det.	I am sure of it.
Hvilken väg reser Herrn härifrån?	What road do you take from hence, Sir?
Jag tänker mig ock til Harwich.	I also intend to go to Harwich.
Låt oss då göra sällskap.	Let us then make a party.
Låt oss resa tilsammans.	Let us go together.
Jag har egen vagn.	I have my own carriage.
Åk med mig.	Travel with me.
Jag är Herrn mycket förbunden.	I am much obliged to you, Sir. Jag

Jag emottager gerna Herrns tilbud.	I gladly accept your offer.
Det är et vackert land.	It is a fine country.
Vägen är ganska god.	The road is very good.
Har Herrn sitt pass?	Have you your passport.
Vi måste upge våra namn.	We must give in our names.
Är allt färdigt?	Is every thing ready?
Fattas ingenting?	Is nothing wanted?
Har Herrn glömt någonting?	Have you forgot any thing?
Är allt betaldt?	Is every thing paid?
Har Herrn liqviderat om fragten?	Have you settled about the freight?
Allt är bestyrdt.	All is arranged.
När ska vi gå om bord?	When are we to go on board?
Strax; detta ögonblick.	Immediately; this moment.
Äro sakerna om bord?	Are the things on board?
Är allt i båten?	Is every thing in the boat?
Kom låt oss gå.	Come let us go.
Har Herrn varit på sjön förut?	Have you been on the sea before?
Jag har varit i Ost-Indien.	I have been in the East-Indies.
Jag har seglat mycket omkring.	I have sailed a good deal about.
Det är vackert väder.	It is fine weather.
Det blåser alldeles icke.	It does not blow at all.

Det begynner blåsa.	It begins to blow.
Vi ha en god vind.	We have a fair wind.
Det blåser hårdt.	It blows hard.
Det ser ut som skulle vi få en storm.	It looks as if we should have a storm.
Det begynner regna.	It begins to rain.
Hör Herrn åskan?	Do you hear the thunder
Det blixtar. Det ljungar.	It lightens.
Blixt; Ljungeld.	Lightning; Flash of light
Thordön; Åskdunder.	Thunder. [ning]
Vi ha refvat seglen.	We have reefed the sails
Stormen har lagt sig.	The storm is laid.
Stormen är förbi; stormen har uphört.	The storm is blown over has ceased.
Vi ha vackert nu.	We have it fine now.
Det är skönt väder.	It is beautiful weather.
Har Herrn en bok at läna mig?	Have you a book to lend me, Sir?
Kan Herrn läna mig en bok?	Can you lend me a book Sir?
Hvilken bok vill Herrn låna?	What book do you wish to borrow?
Jag kan läna Herrn hvilken bok Herrn vill.	I can lend you any book you choose.
Jag ville låna en resbeskrifning.	I wished to borrow a book of travels.
Har Herrn någon sådan?	Have you any such?
Har Herrn någon resbeskrifning öfver Sverige?	Have you any travel through Sweden?

99

Jag har två eller tre til min Herres tjenst.

I have two or three at your service.

Tycker Herrn om resbeskrifningar?

Do you like travels, Sir?

Herrn bör läsa Catteaus beskrifning öfver Sverige.

You should read Catteau's description of Sweden *).

Här är Küttners resa i Danmark och Sverige.

Here is Küttner's travels in Denmark and Sweden †).

Har Herrn Acerbi's resa?

Have you got Acerbi's Travels?

Hvad tycker Herrn om den?

How do you like it?

Om hans upgifter få vi snart tilfälle at dömma.

Concerning his statements we shall soon be able to judge.

Jag har stor anledning at tvifla på deras rigtighet.

I have great reason to doubt the truth of them.

Hans bok är icke väl omtalad i någon jurnal.

His book is not well spoken of in any review.

Hvad har Herrn emot Acerbi?

What have you against Acerbi?

Hans låga sätt at vanställa karakterer, at göra förtjenst och Gudsfruktan misstänkte, och den redliga enfalden löjlig.

His low manner of misrepresenting characters, making merit and piety suspected, and ridiculing honest simplicity.

*) A general view of Sweden, translated from the French.
†) See Collection of Modern and Contemporary Voyages and Travels.

Hvad skepp är det vi se?	What ship is it we see?
Det ser ut som en fregatt.	It looks like a frigate.
Det är et köpmans fartyg.	It is a merchant's vessel.
Ska vi preja det?	Shall we hail it?
Låt oss hissa flaggen.	Let us hoist our colours.
Det tyckes vara djupt lastadt.	It seems to be deep laden.
Det är et Engelskt skepp.	It is an English ship.
Hvarifrån kommer Ni?	Whence do you come?
Jag kommer från Öster-sjön.	I come from the Baltick.
Hvad last har Ni inne?	What cargo have you?
Jag har jern och bräder.	I have iron and deals.
Stål, koppar, tjära.	Steel, copper, tar.
Beck, talg, hampa.	Pitch, tallow, hemp.
Lin, timmer, master.	Flax, timber, masts.
Stäfver och tran.	Staves and train-oil.
Hvart skall Ni gå?	Whither are you bound?
Jag ärnar mig til London.	I am bound for London.
Jag önskar er en lycklig resa.	I wish you a happy voyage.
Har Ni mött någon ka-pare?	Have you met any priva-teer?
Såg ni den stora flottan?	Did you see the large fleet?
Alla skeppen voro i Sun-det.	All the ships were in the Sound.
När lemnade Ni lotsen?	When did you leave the pilot?

förrgårs afton.	In the evening on the day before yesterday.
Har Ni någon fisk?	Have you got any fish?
Låt oss försöka at fiska.	Let us try to fish.
Hvad slags fisk är det?	What kind of fish is that?
Den stora är en torsk.	The large one is a cod.
Hvad kallar Ni denhär?	What do you call this?
Det är en kolja,	It is a haddock,
En flundra,	A flounder,
En tunga, en karp,	A sole, a carp.
En kabiljo,	A codfish,
En sill, en makrill.	A herring, a mackerel.
Har Ni någon hummer?	Have you got any lobsters?
Kräftor och musslor.	Crawfish and muscles.
Låt oss försöka at meta.	Let us try to angle.
Här är en metref.	Here is a fishing line.
Sätt en sill på kroken.	Put a herring on the hook.
Hvad är det vi se?	What is it we see?
Är det land eller moln?	Is it land or clouds?
Vi äro på Svenska kusten.	We are on the Swedish coast.
Det är Svenska landet.	'Tis the Swedish shore.
Hvem kommer der?	Who comes there?
Hvem är i båten?	Who is in the boat?
Det är en fiskarbåt.	It is a fishing boat.
Det är lotsen som kommer.	It is the pilot that comes.
Behöfva vi en lots?	Do we want a pilot?
Kom på däck.	Come on deck.
Det är en hög klippa.	It is a high rock.

Hvad är det för et torn?	What tower is that?
Det är en fästning.	It is a fortress.
Hvar ska vi landa?	Where shall we land?
Låt oss gå i land här.	Let us go a shore here.
Ropa kajut-vakten.	Call the cabin-boy.
Vi måste snygga oss.	We must adjust ourselves
Vi måste kläda oss.	We must dress ourselves
Här är en skål med vatten.	Here is a bason of water
Tag hit tvålen.	Bring the soap here.
Låna mig en rakknif.	Lend me a razor.
Jag kan ej raka mig sjelf.	I cannot shave myself.
Har Herrn tvättat sig?	Have you washed yourself, Sir?
Jag är strax färdig.	I am ready immediately.
Huru många ska ro?	How many shall row?
Kan Herrn visa mig vägen?	Can you show me the way, Sir?
Var så god och säg mig vägen.	Be so kind as to tell me the way.
Jag hittar *) alldeles icke.	I do not know the way at all.
Det är en vacker gata.	It is a fine street.
Hvad är detta för et hus?	What house is this?
Hvem bor här?	Who lives here?
Hvad heter detta ställe?	What is this place called?
Det är et värdshus.	It is a tavern.
Har Ni rum at hyra ut?	Do you let lodgings?

*) *At hitta*, to find, to know the way. *Jag hittar sjelf*, I know the way myself.

Kan jag få bo i ert hus? May I lodge in your house?

Hvad begär Ni i veckan? What do you ask a week?

Hvad skall jag betala? What must I pay?

Bär in mina saker. Bring in my things.

Hvar är min kappsäck? Where is my portmanteau?

Är min koffert der? Is my trunk there?

Jag saknar ingenting. I miss nothing.

Om mat och drick. *About eating & drinking.*

Jag är hungrig. I am hungry.

Jag känner mig hungrig. I feel myself hungry.

Ge mig någonting at äta. Give me something to eat.

Hvad kan jag få at äta? What can I have to eat?

Har Ni någonting färdigt? Have you any thing ready?

Hvad har Ni til middagen? What have you for dinner?

Jag vill ha fisk til förrätt. I will begin with fish.

Låt mig se matsedeln. Let me see the bill of fare?

Ni har ål, gädda och You have eel, pike, and
aborrar. 　　　　pearches.

Vill Herrn ha färsk lax? Would you like fresh sal-
　　　　mon?

Har ni ingen hvitling? Have you no whitings?

Är soppan god? Is the soup good?

Gif mig en tallrik ärt- Bring me a plate of pease-
soppa. 　　　　soup.

Tycker Herrn ej om kött- Don't you like broth,
soppa? 　　　　Sir?

Jag har lust at smaka den. I have a mind to taste it?

Hvad kötträtter har Ni? What meat have you?

Kokadt eller stekt.	Boiled or roasted.
Var god och ge mig et stycke bröd.	I'll thank you for a piece of bread.
Är oxsteken god?	Is the roast-beef good?
Kalfstek, fårstek.	Roast veal, mutton,
Grisstek, lamstek.	Roast pork, lamb.
Vill Herrn smaka puddingen?	Would you taste the pudding, Sir?
Dricker Herrn vin?	Do you drink wine?
Är vinet godt?	Is the wine good?
Ge mig et glas vin.	Let me have a glass of wine.
Äter Herrn rädisor?	Do you eat radishes?
Jag tycker mer om sallaten.	I like the sallad better.
Här är ost, smör.	Here is cheese, butter.
Vill Herrn ha svagdricka eller öl?	Would you have table-beer or ale?
Har ni någon porter?	Have you any porter?
Jag har Stockholms öl.	I have Stockholm's stout-ale.

Om kläder.	About dress.
Skicka efter en skräddare.	Send for a taylor.
Hattmakare, skomakare.	Hatter, shoemaker.
Ni måste göra mig en surtut, en frack, en vest, et par byxor.	You must make me a great coat, a frock, a waistcoat, a pair of breeches.
Hvilken färg skall det bli?	What colour shall it be?

Hvar är profvet? — Where is the pattern?

Hvad kostar hatten? — What does the hat cost?

Behöfver Herrn någonting tvättadt åt sig? — Do you want to have any thing washed for you, Sir?

Här är en tvätterska. — Here is a laundress.

Tag hit en ren halsduk, skjorta, näsduk, strumpor, calesonger. — Bring me a clean neck-cloth, shirt, pocket-handkerchief, stockings, drawers.

Hvar äro mina skor? — Where are my shoes?

Här är et par stöflar. — Here is a pair of boots.

Är hårfrisörn kommen? — Is the hair-dresser come?

Ni måste klippa mitt hår. — You must cut my hair.

En kam, en sax, pomada, puder, tandborste, nageltång. — A comb, a pair of scissars, pomatum, powder, tooth-brush, nail-nippers.

Köp mig et par skoband, et par hängslor. — Buy me a pair of shoe-strings, a pair of slings.

Brukar Herrn spännen? — Do you wear buckles?

Hvar är min käpp och mina handskar? — Where is my stick and my gloves?

Om en resa. — Of a Journey.

När ska vi resa? — When shall we set off?

Du måste beställa hästar. — You must bespeak horses?

Jag har försett mig med löspengar och småsedlar. — I have provided myself with change and small banknotes.

Jag har femton riksdaler i småmynt *).	I have fifteen rixdollars in change.
Huru många hästar behöfva vi?	How many horses do we want?
Hästarne äro förspände.	The horses are put to.
Hvilken väg ska vi ta?	Which road shall we take?
Jag måste taga afsked.	I must take leave.
Kör öfver bron.	Drive over the bridge.
Hur långt är det til nästa håll?	How far is it to the next stage?
Sex fjerdingsväg.	Six quarters of a mile.
En och en half mil ell. halfannan mil **).	One mile and a half.
Hvar står milstolpen? (fjerdingstolpe.)	Where stands the mile-stone?
Kör på. Jag vill gå upför backen.	Drive on. I will walk up the hill.
Kör ej så fort.	Don't drive so fast.
Håll. Låt hästarna stå litet.	Stop. Let the horses stand a little.
Kör fram. Vi äro nu framme.	Drive up. We are now arrived at the place.
Är detta gästgifvargården?	Is this the inn?
Hvar är hållkarlen?	Where is the ostler?

*) Forty-eight Swedish shillings make a rixdollar, besides which there are silver-coins of 32, 16, 8, 4, and 2 shillings. It depends on the course of exchange how many rixdollars of the Bank of Sweden go to a pound sterling — commonly between four and five.

**) We generally count six English miles to one Swedish.

Har ni hästar inne?	Have you horses at hand?
Sätt för genast.	Put them to immediately.
Jag skall skynda mig.	I will make haste.
Hvad har jag at betala?	What have I to pay?
Tre daler *) milen.	Three dollars a mile.
Räknar Ni silfver- eller koppar-dalrar?	Do you count by silver or copper dollars?
Låt oss ge oss af.	Let us set off.
Gaf du några drickspengar?	Did you give any drink-money?
Hvem rår om det huset?	Who is the owner of that house?
Hvem bor der?	Who lives there?
Det hör til Kronan.	It belongs to the King.
Hvar ska vi köra in i staden?	Where shall we put up in town?
Du kör galet.	You drive the wrong way.
Får jag bo hos Er?	May I lodge with you?
Jag behöfver två rum.	I want two rooms.
Jag behöfver en säng-kammare, et förmak.	I want a bed-room, a parlour.
Ni måste koka mig kaffe.	You must make me some coffee.
Téet är färdigt.	The tea is ready.

*) There are eighteen copper- and six silver-dollars to a rixdollar.

A SHORT
VOCABULARY
OF
SUCH WORDS AS ARE IN COMMON USE.

~~~~~~

EXPLANATION OF THE LETTRES AND FIGURES WHICH ARE PLACED
BY THE WORDS.

a. 1, 2, 3, signifies an Active Verb of the 1st, 2d, or 3d Conjugation.

d. 1, 2, 3, — — a Demi Passive Verb of the 1st, 2d, or 3d Conjugation.

i. 1, 2, 3, 4, — — An Irreguler Verb of the 1st, 2d, 3d, or 4th Class.

ad. — — an Adjective.

s. — — a noun used only in the Singular number.

p. — — a Noun used only in the Plural number.

Nos. 1, 2, 3, 4, 5, when standing by nouns, denote their different declensions.

c. masculine or feminine; *n.* neuter

By referring these abbreviations to the Grammar, the reader will easily discover not only the gender of a noun, (whether he must use *en* or *et,* see p. 16) but also what termination he is to give it in the plural number. And in the same manner the inflections of the different verbs may be ascertained by comparing them with the paradigms.

———

ABATE, Slå af *), minska, *a.* Abode, Boning, 2.
Able, Skicklig, *ad.* i stånd. Above, Öfver.
I am able, Jag är i stånd. About, Omkring.

*) *At slå* signifies to beat. It is an irregular Verb of the third class: *Jag slår,* imperf. *Jag slog* (see p. 40) but instead of the participles *slått, slådd, slådt,* we use *slagit, slagen,* and *sloget.*

Abroad, Ute, Utomlands.

Absence, Frånvaro, *s. c.*

Absent, Frånvarande, *ad.*

Abuse, Missbruk 5. ovelt, *s. n.*

Accept, Emottaga. *i.* 2.

Accident, Händelse, 3.

Accuse, Anklaga, *a.* 1.

Ach, Värk, 2, Smärta, 1.

Acknowledge, Erkänna, *a.* 2.

Acquaintance, Bekantskap, 3.

Admittance, Tillträde, 4.

Admonish, Förmana, *a.* 1.

Adorn, Pryda, *a.* 2.

Advance, Försträcka, *a.* 3.

Advantage, Förmån, 3.

Advice, Råd, 5.

Affirm, Bekräfta, *a.* 1.

Afflict, Bedröfva, *a.* 1.

Afraid, Rädd, *ad.*

After, Efter.

Again, Igen.

Age, Ålder, 2.

Agreeable, Angenäm, *ad.*

Ague, Frossa, 1.

Aim, Syfte, 4. Afsigt, 3.

Air, Luft, *s. c.*

Ale, Öl, *s. n.*

Alien, Utländning, 2.

Almost, Nästan.

Alone, Allena.

Also, Också, Ock.

Although, Ehuru.

Altitude, Höjd, 3.

Always, Alltid.

Amiable, Älskvärd, *ad.*

Amicably, Vänligt.

Among, Bland.

Amount, Belopp, 5.

Anchor, Ankar, 5. *n.*

Ancient, Gammal, *ad.*

Angry, Vred, Ond, *ad.*

Anker, Ankare, 5. *c.*

Annual, Årlig, *ad.*

Answer, Svar, 5.

Answer, Svara, *a.* 1.

Ant, Myra, 1.

Anxiety, Oro, *s. c.*

Any, Någon, pl. Några.

Apology, Ursäkt, 3.

Apparel, Klädnad. 3.

Appear, Synas, *d.* 3.

Appearance, Utseende, 4.

Appetite, Matlust, *s. o.*

Apple, Äple, 4.

Appoint, Bestämma, *a.* 2.

Appraise, Värdera, *a.* 1.

Apprehension, Fruktan, *s. c.*

Apprentice, Lärling, 2.

Approach, Nalkas, *d.* 1.

Approve, Gilla, *a.* 1.

Arch, Båge, 2.

Ardent, Ifrig, *ad.*

Arm, Arm, 2.

Arm, Beväpna, *a.* 1.

Armour, Rustning, 2.

Around, Rundtomkring.

Arrive, Ankomma, *i.* 4.

Arrow, Pil, 2.

Art, Konst, 3.

Artist, Konstnär, 3.

Ascend, Upstiga, *i.* 2.

Ashes, Aska, *s. c.*

Ask, Fråga, *a.* 1.

Aspire, Eftersträfva, *a.* 1.

Ass, Åsna, 1.

Assassin, Mördare, 5.

Assert, Bekräfta, *a.* 1.

Assist, Bistå, *i.* 3.

Assistance, Bistånd, 5.

As soon as, Så snart som.

Assure, Försäkra, *a.* 1.

Attachment, Tilgifvenhet.

Attain, Upnå, *a.* 2.

Attendant, Medfölje, 4.

Attentive, Upmärksam, *ad.*

Attest, Betyga, *a.* 1.

Attorney, Advokat, 3.

Aught, Något.

Aunt, Faster, Moster, 2.

Austral, Sydlig, *ad.*

Autumn, Höst, 2.

Average, Haveri, 3.

Avow, Tilstå, *i.* 3.

Awake, Vaken, *ad.*

Awake, Väcka, *a.* 3.

Baby, Litet barn.

Bachelor, Ungkarl, 2.

Bacon, Fläsk, *s. n.*

Bad, Elak, *ad.*

Bag, Säck, Påse, 2.

Bail, Borgen, *s. c.*

To bail, Gå i borgen.

Baker, Bagare, 5.

Ball, Boll, 2. Bal, 3.

Banish, Förvisa, *a.* 3.

Bar, Rigel, Disk, 2.

Bargain, Köp, 5.

Barge, Slup, 2.

Barrel, Tunna, 1.

Base, Nedrig, *ad.*

Basket, Korg, 2.

Bay, Hafsvik, 2.

Beam, Bjelke, Sparre, 2.

Beard, Skägg, *s. n.*

Beat, Slå, *i.* 2.

Beauty, Skönhet, 3.

Bee, Bi, 4.

Beer, Dricka, *s. n.*

Before, För, Förut.

Beg, Begära, *a.* 2.

Beggar, Tiggare, 5.

Begin, Begynna, *a.* 3.

Behaviour, Upförande, *s. n.*

Belief, Tro, *s. c.*
Believe, Tro, *a.* 2.
Bell, Klocka, 1.
Belong, Höra til.
Below, Nedom.
Bend, Böja, *a.* 2.
Berry, Bär, 5.
Bespeak, Beställa, *a.* 2.
Bet, Vad, 5.
Between, Emellan.
Bible, Bibel, 2.
Big, Stor, Tjock, *ad.*
Bill, Räkning, Sedel, 2.
Bill of fare, Matsedel, 2.
Billow, Bölja, 1.
Bind, Binda, *i.* 2.
Bird, Fågel, 2.
Black, Svart, *ad.*
Blanket, Filt, 2.
Bleed, Blöda, *a.* 2.
Bless, Välsigna, *a.* 1.
Bliss, Sällhet, 3.
Blood, Blod, *s. c.*
Blow, Slag, Hugg, 5.
Blow, Blåsa, *a.* 3.
Blue, Blå, *ad.*
Boast, Skryta, *i.* 2.
Body, Kropp, 2.
Boil, Koka, *a.* 1.
Bolt, Rigel, Bom, 2.
Bonnet, Mössa, 1.

Bore, Nafvare, 5.
Borrow, Låna, *a.* 1. 3.
Boundary, Gräns, 3.
Bounty, Värfning, 2.
Box, Ask, 2. Låda, 1.
Boy, Gosse, Pojke, 2.
Brain, Hjerna, 1.
Brandy, Cognac, *s. c.*
Swedish Brandy, Bränvin, *s. o.*
Bread, Bröd, 5.
Break, Bryta, *i.* 2.
Breakfast, Frukost, 2.
Breeches, Byxor, *p.*
Brick, Tegel, 5.
Bride, Brud, 2.
Bridge, Bro, 2.
Bridle, Töm, Tygel, 2.
Bring, Bringa, *i.* 4.
Brisk, Frisk, *ad.*
Broad, Bred, *ad.*
Broker, Mäklare, 5.
Brook, Bäck, 2.
Brown, Brun, *ad.*
Brush, Borste, 2.
Buckle, Spänne, 4.
Bundle, Bunt, 2.
Buoy, Ankarboj, 2.
Burden, Börda, 1.
Burial, Begrafning, 2.
Burn, Brinna, *i.* 1.
Burn, Bränna, *a.* 2.

Bush, Buske, 2.

Butter, Smör, *s. n.*

Buy, Köpa, *a.* 3.

By, Vid, Genom.

By-and-by, Rättnu.

Cabin, Kajuta, 1.

Cable, Ankartåg, 5.

Cage, Fågelbur, 2.

Calf, Kalf, 2. Vada, 1.

Call, Ropa, Kalla, *a.* 1.

Calling, Embete, 4. Kall, 5.

Calm, Lugn, Stilla, *ad.*

Candle, Ljus, 5.

Candlestick, Ljusstake, 2.

Cap, Mössa, 1.

Capacity, Skicklighet, 3.

Capital, Hufvudstad, 3.

Captain, Capten, 3.

Captive, Fånge, 2.

Card, Kort, 5. Karda, 1.

Care, Omsorg, 3. Akt, *s. c.*

Careful, Aktsam, *ad.*

Carpet, Golfmatta, 1.

Carrot, Morot, 3.

Cart, Kärra, 1.

Cash, Contant, 3.

Castle, Slott, 5.

Cause, Orsak, 3.

Cautious, Försigtig, *ad.*

Cave, Håla, 1. Grop, 2.

Cease, Uphöra, *a.* 2.

Certain, Viss, *ad.*

Certainly, Visserligen.

Certainty, Visshet, *s. c.*

Chace, Jagt, 3.

Chair, Stol, 2.

Chalk, Krita, *s. c.*

Chamber, Kammare, 5.

Chance, Händelse, 3.

Change, Vexel, 2.

Change, Vexla, *a.* 1.

Channel, Kanal, 3.

Charcoal, Kol, 5.

Charm, Intaga, *i.* 2.

Chaste, Kysk, *ad.*

Cheap, Billig, *ad.*

Cheat, Bedrägeri, 3.

Cheerful, Munter, *ad.*

Cheese, Ost, 2.

Cherry, Kersbär, 5.

Chew, Tugga, *a.* 1.

Chicken, Kyckling, 2.

Child, Barn, 5.

Chill, Kyla, *s. c.*

Chimney, Spis, Skorsten, 2.

Choice, Val, 5.

Choose, Välja, *a.* 2.

Do you choose? Befallen J?

Christmas, Jul, 2.

Church, Kyrka, 1.

Cinnamon,

Cinnamon, Kanel, *s. c.*
Circle, Cirkel, 2.
Circumstance, Omständig-
Citizen, Borgare, 5. [het, 3.
City, Stad, 3.
Civil, Höflig, *ad.*
Claim, Anspråk, 5.
Claw, Klo, 3.
Clean, Ren, *ad.*
Clear, Klar, *ad.*
Cloak, Kappa, 1.
Clock, Klocka, 1. Ur, 5.
Close, Sluta, Afsluta, *a.* 1.
Cloth, Kläde, 4.
Clothes, Kläder, *p.*
Cloud, Moln, 5.
Coach, Vagn, 2.
Coachman, Kusk, 2.
Coal, Stenkol, 5.
Coarse, Grof, *ad.*
Coast, Kust, 3.
Coat, Rock, 2.
Coin, Mynt, 5.
Cold, Kall, *ad.* Köld, *s. c.*
Get a cold, Få en förkylning.
Colour, Färg, 3.
Colours, Flagga, Fana, 1.
Comb, Kam, 2.
Come, Komma, *i.* 4.
Comfort, Tröst, *s. c.*
Common, Allmän, *ad.*

Common, Allmänning, 2.
Company, Sällskap, 5.
Compass, Compass, *s. o.*
Compassion, Medlidande, 4.
Compel, Tvinga, *i.* 1.
Competency, Utkomst, *s. c.*
Conceal, Fördölja, *a.* 2.
Conduct, Upförande, *s. n.*
Confidence, Förtroende, 4.
Congregation, Församling, 2.
Conquest, Eröfring, 2.
Conscience, Samvete, 4.
Consent, Bifall, 5.
Consist, Bestå, *i.* 3.
Consult, Rådfråga, *a.* 1.
Consume, Förtära, *a.* 2.
Contain, Innehålla, *i.* 2.
Continent, Fast land.
Contrive, Utfinna, *i.* 1.
Convict, Öfverbevisa, *a.* 3.
Copper, Koppar, *s. c.*
Corn, Korn, 5. Liktorn, 2.
Corner, Hörn, 5.
Cost, Kosta, *a.* 1. Kostnad, 3.
Count, Räkna, *a.* 1.
Country, {
  Land, *pl.* Länder.
  Fädernesland, *s. n.*
  Fosterland, *s. n.*
  Fosterjord, *s. c.*
  Fosterbygd, *s. c.*
}
Couple, Et par.

Cow, Ko, 3.

Cow-pock, Skyddskoppor, *p.*

Crack, Knäppa, *a.* 3.

Cream, Grädda, *s. c.*

Creator, Skapare.

Creature, Kreatur, 5.

Creep, Krypa, Smyga, *i.* 2.

Crew, Besättning, 2.

Crowd, Folkhop, 2.

Cruel, Grym, *ad.*

Cruelty, Grymhet, 3.

Cruise, Kryssa, *a.* 1.

Crush, Krossa, *a.* 1.

Crust, Skorpa, 1.

Cry, Ropa, *a.* 1. Gråta, *i.* 2.

Cunning, Listig, *ad.*

Cup, Kopp, 2.

Cure, Kur, 3.

Currants, Vinbär, 5.

Curtain, Gardin, 3.

Custom, Vana, 1. Tull, 2.

Customhouse, Tullhus, 5.

Cut, Skära, *i.* 1.

Daily, Daglig, *ad.* Dagligen.

Damage, Skada, *a.* 1.

Damp, Fuktig, *ad.*

Danger, Fara, 1.

Dare, Våga, *a.* 1.

Dark, Mörk, *ad.*

Dawn, Dagas, *d.* 1.

Day, Dag, 2.

Dead, Död, *ad.*

Deaf, Döf, *ad.*

Deal, Bräde, 4. Del, 2.

Deal, Dela, *a.* 1.

Dear, Dyr, *ad.*

Death, Död, 2.

Debt, Skuld, 3.

Deceit, Bedrägeri, 3.

Deceive, Bedraga, *i.* 2.

Decent, Anständig, *ad.*

Decide, Afgöra, *a.* 2.

Deck, Däck.

Declare, Förklara, *a.* 1.

Decline, Afböja, *a.* 2.

Decree, Beslut, 5.

Deduct, Afdraga, *i.* 2.

Deem, Dömma, *a.* 2.

Deep, Djup, *ad.*

Deer, Hjort, 2.

Defect, Fel, 5. Brist, 3.

Defence, Försvar, 5.

Defend, Försvara, *a.* 1.

Defer, Upskjuta, *i.* 2.

Defray, Betala, *a.* 3.

Defy, Trotsa, *a.* 1.

Degree, Grad, 3.

Delay, Dröja, *a.* 2.

Delight, Förnöjelse, 3.

Deliver, Befria, *a.* 1.

Demand, Påstående, 4.

Demand, Fordra, *a.* 1.

Deny, Neka, *a.* 1.

Depend, Lita (på), *a.* 1.

Depth, Djup, 5.

Desart, Ödemark, 3.

Descend, Nedstiga, *i.* 2.

Deserve, Förtjena, *a.* 3.

Design, Afsigt, 3.

Desire, Åstundan, *s. c.*

Destiny, Bestämmelse, 3.

Destroy, Förstöra, *a.* 2.

Detain, Qvarhålla, *i.* 2.

Detect, Uptäcka, *a.* 3.

Determination, Beslut, 5.

Detest, Afsky, *a.* 2.

Devotion, Andakt, *s. c.*

Dew, Dagg, *s. c.*

Dial, Solvisare, 5.

Die, Dö, *i.* 3.

Direct, Ställa, *a.* 2.

Dirt, Smuts, *s. c.*

Discharge, Afskeda, *a.* 1.

Disease, Sjukdom, 2.

Displease, Misshaga, *a.* 1.

Distance, Afstånd, 5.

Distant, Aflägsen, *ad.*

Distress, Nöd, *s. c.*

Disturb, Oroa, *a.* 1.

Ditch, Dike, 4.

Dive, Dyka, *a.* 1.

Divide, Dela, *a.* 1. 3.

Divine, Gudomlig, *ad.*

Do, Göra, *a.* 2.

Dog, Hund, 2.

Door, Dörr, 2.

Down, Dun, 5.

Down, Ned.

Dram, Qvintin, 5. Sup, 2.

Draught, Dryck, 3.

Draw, Draga, *i.* 2.

Dreadful, Förskräcklig, *ad.*

Dream, Dröm, 2.

Dress, Kläda, *a.* 2.

Dress, Klädnad, 3.

Drink, Dricka, *i.* 1.

Droll, Löjlig, *ad.*

Drum, Trumma, 1.

Drunk, Drucken, *ad.*

Dry, Torr, *ad.* Torka, *a.* 1.

Duck, And. *pl.* Änder.

Duke, Hertig, 2.

Dusk, Skymning, *s. c.*

Dust, Stoft, Dam, *s. n.*

Dusty, Dammig, *ad.*

Duty, Skyldighet, 3.

Dwell, Bo, *a.* 2.

Dye, Färg, 3.

Each, Hvarje.

Ear, Öra, *pl.* Öron.

Early, Tidigt.

Earn, Förtjena, *a.* 1.

Earnest, Allvar, *s. n.*

Earth, Jord, *s. c.*

Earthenware, Krukkärl, 5.

Ease, Lätta, Lindra, *a.* 1.

Easy, Lätt, *ad.*

Eat, Äta, *imperf.* Åt.

Eclipse, Förmörkelse, 3.

Eel, Ål, 2.

Egg, Egg, 5.

Elbow, Armbåge, 2.

Elk, Elg, 2.

Eloquent, Vältalig, *ad.*

Else, Annars.

Emancipation, Frigörelse, 3.

Embark, Gå om bord.

Emetic, Kräkmedel, 5.

Eminence, Höjd, Höghet, 3.

Emperor, Kejsare, 5.

Empty, Tom, *ad.* Töma, *a.* 2.

Enable, Sätta i stånd.

End, Slut, Ändamål, 5.

Endless, Oändelig, *ad.*

Engine, Spruta, 1.

Enjoyment, Njutning, 2.

Ensign, Fändrik, 2.

Ensure, Assecurera, *a.* 1.

Enter, Gå in.

Entry, Förstuga, 1.

Equinox, Dagjemning, 2.

Evade, Undfly, *a.* 2.

Even, Äfven.

Evening, Afton, 2.

Event, Händelse, 3.

Ever, Alltid.

Evil, Ond, *ad.*

Exalted, Uphöjd, *ad.*

Excell, Öfverträffa, *a.* 1.

Except, Undantaga, *s.* 2.

Exception, Undantag, 5.

Exchange, Börs, 2.

Exchequer, Rentkammare, 5.

Excite, Upväcka, *a.* 3.

Exclude, Utsluta, *s.* 2.

Excuse, Ursäkt, 3.

Exertion, Bemödande, 4.

Exhort, Upmuntra, *a.* 1.

Exorbitant, Öfverdrifven, *ad.*

Expect, Vänta, *a.* 1.

Expectation, Väntan, *s. c.*

Expedient, Utväg, 2.

Explain, Förklara, *a.* 1.

Expose, Utsätta, *s.* 4.

Express, Uttrycka, *a.* 3.

Extend, Utsträcka, *a.* 3.

External, Utvertes.

Extinguish, Utsläcka, *a.* 3.

Extract, Utdraga, *s.* 2.

Extreamly, Ganska.

Extricate, Utveckla, *a.* 1.

Eye, Öga, *pl.* Ögon.

Eyebrow, Ögonbryn, 5.

Eyelid, Ögonlock.

Face, Ansigte, 4.

Fact, Verk, 5. Gerning, 2.

Fade, Förvissna, *a.* 1.

Fagot, Risknippa, 1.

Faint, Svag, Matt, *ad.*

Fair, Vacker, Täck, *ad.*

Fair, Marknad, 3.

Faith, Tro, *s. c.* Lära, 1.

Faithfull, Trogen, *ad.*

Fall, Fall, 5. Falla, *i.* 2.

False, Falsk, *ad.*

Fame, Rygte, 4.

Famine, Hungersnöd, *s. c.*

Famous, Rygtbar, *ad.*

Fancy, Tycke, 4.

Far, Långt, *How far?* hur

Farm, Arrende-jord. [*långt?*

Farrier, Hofslagare, 5.

Farther, Längre,

Fast, Fort.

Fat, Fet, *ad.*

Fate, Öde, 4.

Father, Fader, *pl.* Fäder.

Fathom, Famn, 2.

Fault, Fel, 5.

Fear, Fruktan, *s. c.*

Feather, Fjäder, 2.

Fee, Lön, 3. Arfode, 4.

Fees, Drickspengar.

Feel, Känna, *a.* 2.

Feeling, Känsla, 1.

Fellon, Missdådare, 5.

Ferry, Färja, 1. Färja, *a.* 1.

Fertile, Fruktbar, *ad.*

Fetch, Hemta, *a.* 1.

Fetters, Fjättrar, *p,*

Fever, Feber, 2.

Few, Få, *comp.* Färre.

Fickle, Ostadig, *ad.*

Field, Fält, 5. Mark, 3.

Fig, Fikon, 5.

Fight, Batalj, 3.

Fight, Strida, *a.* 2. Slåss (p. 74)

Fill, Fylla, *a.* 2.

Final, Slutlig, *ad.*

Fine, Fin, Skön, *ad.*

Finger, Finger, 2.

Finish, Sluta, *a.* 1.

Fir, Furuträd, 5. Tall, 2.

Fire, Eld, 2.

Fireside, Brasa, 1.

Fish, Fisk, 2. Fiska, *a.* 1.

Fit, Passande, Beqväm, *ad.*

Fix, Fästa, *a.* 1.

Flame, Låga, 1.

Flannel, Flanell, 3.

Flap, Upslag, 5.

Flat, Flat, Platt, Slät, *ad.*

Flax, Lin, *s. n.*

Flea, Loppa, 1.

Fleet, Flotta, 1.

Flesh, Kött, *s. n.*

Flexible, Böjlig, *ad.*

Flight, Flygt, Flykt, *s. c.*

Fling, Kasta, *a.* 1.

Float, Flyta, *i.* 2. Drifta, *a.* 1.

Flog, Piska, *a.* 1.

Flood, Flod, 3.

Floor, Golf, 5.

Flour, Mjöl, *s. n.*

Flow, Flyta, *i.* 2. Rinna, *i.* 1.

Flower, Blomma, 1.

Fly, Fluga, 1.

Fly, Fly, *a.* 2. Flyga, *i.* 2.

Fog, Dimma, 1.

Fold, Lägga (*i.* 4.) ihop.

Follow, Följa, *a.* 2.

Folly, Dårskap, 3.

Food, Mat, Föda, *s. c.*

Fool, Narr, Tok, 2.

Foot, Fot, *pl.* Fötter, 3.

Forbid, Förbjuda, *i.* 2.

Forehead, Panna, 1.

Foreigner, Utländning, 2.

Forfeit, Förverka, *a.* 1.

Forge, Smedja, 1. Smida, *a.* 2.

Forgery, Förfalskning, 2.

Forget, Förgäta, *i.* 2. Glöm-

Forgive, Förlåta, *i.* 2. [ma.

Fort, Skans, Fästning, 2.

Fortune, Lycka, Rikedom, 2.

Foul, Ful, Skamlig, *ad.*

Foundation, Grundval, 2.

Foundling, Hittebarn, 5.

Fountain, Källa, 1.

Fowl, Höns, 5.

Fox, Räf, 2.

Frame, Ram, 2.

France, Frankrike.

Fraternity, Brorskap, 5.

Fraud, Svek, 5. Bedrägeri, 3.

Free, Fri, *ad.*

Freeze, Frysa, *i.* 2.

Freight, Fragt, 3. Laddning,

Freight, Fragta, *a.* 1. [2.

Frequent, Vanlig, *ad.*

Frequent, Besöka, *a.* 3.

Fresh, Färsk, Ny, *ad.*

Friend, Vän, 3. Qväkare, 5.

Friendship, Vänskap, *s. c.*

Fright, Förskräckelse, *s. c.*

Fright, Förskräcka, *a.* 3.

Fringe, Frans, 2.

Frog, Groda, 1.

From, Från.

Frugal, Sparsam, *ad.*

Fruit, Frukt, 3.

Fry, Steka (*a.* 3.) i panna.

Frying pan, Stekpanna, 1.

Fulfil, Fullgöra, *a.* 2.

Fully, Fullkomligen.

Fume, Ånga, 1.

Fun, Skämt, 5. Lek, 2.

Funeral, Likfärd, 3.

Furious, Rasande, *ad.*

Furnace, Ugn, Masugn, 2.

Furnish, Förskaffa, *a.* 1.

Furr, Pelsverk, 5.

Further, Vidare.

Further, Befordra,

Future, Tilkommande, *ad.*

Gain, Vinst, 3. Vinna, *i.* 1.

Gale, Blåst, *s. c.*

Gall, Galla, *s. c.*

Gallows, Galge, 2.

Game, Spel, 5.

Game, (Birds) Vildt, *s. c.*

Garden, Trädgård, 2.

Garment, Klädning, 2.

Garret, Vindskammare, 5.

Garrison, Garnison, 3.

Garter, Strumpband, 5.

Gate, Port, Ingång, 2.

Gather, Samla, *a.* 1.

Gay, Glad, Munter, *ad.*

Generous, Ädelmodig, *ad.*

Gently, Sakta.

Genuine, Oförfalskad, *ad.*

German, Tysk, *ad.*

Ghost, Ande, 2.

Holy Ghost, Den Helige An-

Giddy, Yr, *ad.*   [*de.*

Gift, Gåfva, 1.

Gilt, Förgyld, *ad.*

Ginger, Ingefära, *s. c.*

Girdle, Gördel, 2.

Girl, Flicka, 1.

Give, Gifva, *imp.* Gaf.

Glass, Glas, 5.

Glaze, Glasera, *a.* 1.

Gloomy, Mörk, Dyster, *ad.*

Glory, Ära, *s. c.* Pris, *s. n.*

Gloss, Glans, *s. c.*

Glove, Handske, 2.

Glue, Lim, *s. n.*

Gnat, Mygg, 2.

Goal, Fängelse, 4.

God, Gud, 2.

Gold, Guld, *s. n.*

Good, God, *ad.*

Goods, Gods, *s. n.* Egendom, 2.

Goose, Gås, *pl.* Gäss.

Gooseberry, Krusbär, 5.

Gospel, Evangelium.

Gout, Gikt, *s. c.*

Gown, Klädning, 2.

Night-gown, Nattrock, 2.

Grace, Nåd, *s. c.* Bön, 3.

Grain, Korn, 5.

Grape, Vindrufva, 1.

Grasp, Gripa, *i.* 2.

Grass, Gräs, *s. n.*

Grater, Rifjern, 5. Rasp, 2.

Grave, Graf, 2.

Grave, Allvarsam, *ad.*

Gravel, Grus, Klappersten, 2.

Gravy, Steksaft, 3.

Grease, Smörja, 1. Fett, *s. n.*

Great, Stor, *comp.* Större.

Greedy, Snål, Sniken, *ad.*

Green, Grön, *ad.*

Greens, Grönsaker, *p.*

Grey, Grå, *ad.*

Grief, Sorg, 3. Oro, *s. c.*

Grieve, Sörja, *a.* 2.

Groan, Sucka, Pusta, *a.* 1.

Grocer, Kryddkrämare, 5.

Groin, Ljumske, 2.

Groom, Stalldräng, 2.

Grow, Växa, *a.* 3. Blifva.

Gruel, Hafresoppa, 1.

Guard, Vakt, 3. Vakta, *a.* 1.

Guess, Gissa, *a.* 1.

Guest, Gäst, 3.

Guide, Leda, *a.* 2.

Guilt, Brott, 5.

Guilty, Brottslig, *ad.*

Guittar, Citra, 1.

Gulf, Hafsvik, 2. Afgrund, 3.

Gum, Kåda, *s. c.* Gom, 2.

Gums, Tandkött, 5.

Gun, Bössa, 1. Kanon, 3.

Gunpowder, Krut, *s. n.*

Gypsy, Spåkärng, 2.

Habit, Vana, 1. Klädning, 2.

Hackney-coach, Hyrvagn, 2.

Hail, Hagel, 5.

Hair, Hår, 5.

Hall, Sal, 2.

Ham, Skinka, 1.

Hand, Hand, *pl.* Händer.

Handkerchief, Näsduk, 2.

Handle, Skaft, 5.

Handsome, Vacker, *ad.*

Handspike, Båtshake, 2.

Hang, Hänga, *a.* 2.

Hansel, Handsöl, *s. n.*

Happen, Hända, Råka, *a.* 1.

It happen'd, Det hände.

I happen'd, Jag råkade.

Happy, Lycklig, Säll, *ad.*

Happiness, Sällhet, 3.

Harbour, Hamn, 2.

Hard, Hård, Svår, *ad.*

Harden, Härda, *a.* 1.

Hardly, Svårligen, Knappt.

Hardship, Svårighet, 3.

Hare, Hare, 2.

Harm, Harm, *s. c.* Oförrätt, 3.

Harness, Sele, 2.

Harrow, Harf, 2.

Harvest, Skörd, 2.

Haste, Hast, *s. c.*

Hat, Hatt, 2.

Hate, Hat, *s. n.*

Haughty, Högfärdig, *ad.*

Hawk, Hök, 2.

Hay, Hö, s. n.

Hazy, Töcknig, Fuktig, ad.

Head, Hufvud, 5.

Headach, Hufvudvärk, s. a.

Heal, Hela, Bota, a. 1.

Health, Helsa, s. c.

To your good health, Skål!

Heap, Hop, 2.

Hear, Höra, a. 2.

Hearken, Lyssna, a. 1.

Heart, Hjerta, 4.

Hearty, Frisk, Rask, ad.

Heat, Hetta, s. c.

Heave, Häfva, a. 2. Lyfta, a. 1.

Heaven, Himmel, 2.

Heavy, Tung, Svår, ad.

Hedge, Häck, 2.

Heedless, Vårdslös, ad.

Heel, Häl, Klack, 2.

Height, Höjd, 3. Topp, 2.

Heir, Arfving, 2.

Helm, Styre, 4. Roder, 5.

Help, Hjelp, s. c. Hjelpa, a. 3.

Hem, Fåll, 2. Fålla, a. 1.

Hen, Höna, 1.

Hence, Härifrån.

Heps, Nypon, 5.

Herb, Ört, 3.

Here, Här.

Hero, Hjelte, 2.

Hide, Hud, 2.

Hide, Gömma, a. 2.

High, Hög, ad.

Hinder, Hindra, a. 1.

Hint, Vink, 2.

Hire, Hyra, 1. Hyra, a. 2.

Hoarse, Hes, ad.

Hog, Galt, 2. Svin, 5.

Hoist, Hissa, a. 1.

Hold, Fäste, 4. Hålla, s. 2.

Hole, Hål, 5. Håla, 1.

Holy, Helig, ad.

Home, Hem, 5.

At home, Hemma.

Honest, Ärlig, ad.

Hoof, Hästhof, 2.

Hook, Hake, Krok, 2.

Hoop, Tunnband, 5.

Hops, Humle, s. o.

Hope, Hopp, s. n.

Horse, Hästarna, 2.

Hot, Het, ad.

Hour, Time, 2.

House, Hus, 5.

Hug, Omfamna, a. 1.

Hulk, Skråf (af et skepp) 5.

Hull, Rum (i et skepp) 5.

Humble, Ödmjuk, ad.

Hungry, Hungrig, ad.

Hunt, Jaga, a. 1.

Hurricane, Orkan, 3.

Hurry, Brådska, Hast, *s. c.*
Hurt, Skada, *s.c.* Skada, *a.* 1.
Husband, Man, *pl.* Männer.
Hush, Nedtysta, *a.* 1.
Hut, Koja, 1.
Huzza! Hurra!
Hymn, Psalm, Låfsång.

Ice, Is, 2.
Idle, Lat, Vårdslös, *ad.*
Idol, Afgud, 2.
If, Om.
Ignorance, Okunnighet, *s. c.*
Ill, Sjuk, *ad.*
Illegal, Olaglig, *ad.*
Illness, Sjukdom, 2.
Image, Bild, 3.
Imitate, Efterapa, *a.* 1.
Immense, Omätlig, *ad.*
Immortal, Odödlig, *ad.*
Immovable, Orörlig, *ad.*
Impart, Meddela, *a.* 1.
Impartial, Opartisk, *ad.*
Impatience, Otålighet, *s. c.*
Impediment, Hinder, 5.
Imperfect, Ofullkomlig, *ad.*
Impertinence, Näsvishet, *s.c.*
Impiety, Ogudaktighet, *s. c.*
Importance, Betydenhet, *s.c.*
Imposition, Bedrägeri, 3.
Impression, Intryck, 5.

Improbable, Oliklig, *ad.*
Improper, Otilbörlig, *ad.*
Improve, Förbättra, *a.* 1.
Impudence, Oförskämdhet.
Impunity, Strafflöshet, *s. c.*
Impure, Oren, *ad.*
Inattention, Oaktsamhet, 3.
Incapable, Oduglig, *ad.*
Inch, Tum, *pl.* Tum, *c.*
Incision, Inskärning, 2.
Income, Inkomst, 3.
Increase, Tilväxa, *a.* 3.
Incredible, Otrolig, *ad.*
Incurable, Obotlig, *ad.*
Indeed, I sanning.
Indisposed, Opasslig, *ad.*
Induce, Förmå, *a.* 2.
Inexhaustible, Outöslig, *ad.*
Infamous, Nedrig, *ad.*
Infant, Barn, 5.
Infection, Smitta, 1.
Inferior, Sämre, Lägre.
Infinite, Oändelig.
Infirm, Svag, Utlefvad, *a. d.*
Inflexible, Oböjlig, *ad.*
Inform, Underrätta, *a.* 1.
Infuse, Ingjuta, *i.* 2.
Ingenious, Qvick, Slug, *ad.*
Ingraft, Inympa, *a.* 1.
Ingrave, Gravera, *a.* 1.
Inhabitant, Invånare, 5.

Injection, Insprutning, 2.

Ink, Bläck, *s. n.*

Inkhorn, Bläckhorn.

Inlet, Öppning, 2.

Inmost, Innerst.

Inn, Skjutsgård, 2.

Innocent, Oskyldig, *ad.*

Inoculate, Ympa, *a.* 1.

Inquire, Efterfråga, *a.* 1.

Inquisitive, Frågvis, *ad.*

Insensible, Känslolös, *ad.*

Insert, Införa, *a.* 2.

Insist, Påstå, *i.* 3.

Insolent, Oförskämd, *ad.*

Install, Installera, *a.* 1.

Instance, Exempel, 5.

Instantly, Strax.

Instead, I stället.

Institute, Inrätta, *a.* 1.

Insult, Förolämpa, *a.* 1.

Insure, Assekurera, *a.* 1.

Intend, Ärna, *a.* 1.

Intention, Afsigt.

Interior, Inre.

Internal, Invertes.

Interpret, Uttolka, *a.* 1.

Interr, Begrafva, *i.* 2.

Interrupt, Afbryta, *i.* 2.

Interval, Mellantid, 3.

Interview, Möte, 4.

Intimate, Förtrolig, *ad.*

Intimidate, Skräma, *a.* 2.

Intire, Hel och hållen.

Intirely, Helt och hållet.

Into, Uti.

Intreat, Bönfalla, Anhålla.

Intrenchment, Förskansning.

Invent, Upfinna, *i.* 1.

Invoice, Faktura, 1.

Iron, Jern, *s n.* (raw metal).

Iron, Jern, 5. (manufactured).

Iron-monger, Jernkrämare.

Irresistible, Oemotståndelig.

Irritate, Ägga, Upreta, *a.* 1.

Island, Ö, 2.

Itch, Skabb, Klåda, *s. c.*

Item, Så ock.

Ivory, Elfenben, 5.

Jack, (Boot) Stöfvelknekt, 2.

Jacket, Tröja, Jacka, 1.

Jaundice, Gulsot, *s. c.*

Jaw, Käft, Kindbåge, 2.

Jay, Kaja, 1.

Jest, Skämt, 5.

Jew, Jude, 2.

Jewel, Juvel, 3.

Join, Förena, *a.* 1.

Joiner, Snickare, 5.

Joke, Skämt, 5.

Jolly, Lustig, Rolig, *ad.*

Journey, Resa, 1. (by land).

Joy, Glädje, *s. c.*

Judge, Domare, 5.

Judgment, Urskillning, *s. c.*

Jug, Krus, 5.

Juice, Saft, 3.

Jump, Hopp, 5. Hoppa, *a.* 1.

Jury, Nämnd, 3.

Justice, Rättvisa, *s. c.*

Justly, Rättmätigt.

Kay, Kaj, *s. c.*

Keel, Köl, 2.

Keen, Skarp, Hvass, *ad.*

Keep, Hålla, Behålla, *i.* 2.

Kernel, Kärna 1. och Kärne 2.

Kettle, Kittel, 2.

Key, Nyckel, 2.

Kick, Sparka, *a.* 1.

Kidney, Njure, 2.

Kill, Döda, Slagta, *a.* 1.

Kind, God, Huld, Öm, *ad.*

Kindness, Godhet, Huldhet.

King, Konung, Kung, 2.

Kiss, Kyss, 2. Kyssa, *a.* 3.

Kitchen, Kök, 5.

Kitten, Kattunge, 2.

Knapsack, Kappsäck, 2.

Knee, Knä, 4.

Knife, Knif, 2.

Knight, Riddare, 5.

Knit, Knyta, *i.* 2. Sticka, *i.* 1.

Knock, Slå, *i.* 3. Knacka, *a.* 1.

Knot, Knut, 2.

Know, Veta, *i.* 4. Känna, *a.* 2.

Knowledge, Kunskap, 3.

Knuckle, Knöl, 2.

Labour, Arbete, 4. Verk.

Lace, Spets, 2. Snöre, 4.

Lad. Gosse, 2.

Ladder, Stege, 2.

Ladle, Slef, 2.

Lady, Fru, 2. Fruntimmer, 5.

Lake, Sjö, Insjö, 2.

Lame, Lam, Ofärdig, *ad.*

Lamp, Lampa, 1.

Land, Land, 5. Landa, *a.* 1.

Lane, Gränd, 3.

Language, Språk, 5.

Lanthorn, Lykta, 1.

Lap, Sköte, *s. n.* Knä, 4.

Larboard, Babord.

Lard, Ister, *s. n.*

Larder, Skafferi, 3.

Large, Stor, *ad.*

Lark, Lärka, 1.

Lash, Slag, Hugg, 5.

Late, Sen, *ad.*

Laugh, Skratta, *a.* 1.

Law, Lag, 2.

Lawful, Laglig, *ad.*

Lazy, Lat, Trög, *ad.*

Leach, Blodigel, 2.

Lead, Bly, *s. u.*

Leaf, Löf, 5.

Leakage, Läckage, *s. n.*

Leaky, Otät, Läckig, *ad.*

Lean, Mager, *ad.*

Lean, Luta, *a.* 1.

Learn, Lära, Höra, *a.* 2.

Least, Minst.

Leather, Läder, 5.

Leave, Afsked, Lof, 5.

Leave, Lemna, *a.* 1.

Lee, Lä, *s. n.*

Left, Venster.

Lefthand, Venstra handen.

Leg, Ben, 5. Lägg, 2.

Legal, Laglig, *ad.*

Leisure, Ledighet, *s. e.*

Lemon, Citron, 3.

Lend, Låna, 1. 3.

Length, Längd, 3.

Less, Mindre.

Lessen, Minska, *a.* 1.

Lesson, Lexa, 1. Lärdom, 2.

Letter, Bokstaf, 3. Bref, 5.

Level, Jemn, Slät, *ad.*

Levy, Utskrifning, 2.

Liberty, Frihet, 3.

Library, Bibliotek, 3. 3.

Lick, Slicka, *a.* 1. Slå, *i.* 2.

Life, Lif, 5.

Lift, Lyfta, *a.* 1.

Light, Lätt, Ljus, *ad.*

Light, Ljus, Sken, 5.

Light, Lysa, *a.* 3.

Lighten, Blixtra, Ljunga, *a.* 1.

Lighten, (Ease) Lätta, *a.* 1.

Lightning, Blixt, 2. Ljungeld, •

Like, Lik, *ad.* Lika, *a.* 1. |2.

Likeness, Likhet, *s. e.*

Limb, Lem, 2.

Lime, Kalk, *s. c.*

Limp, Halta, *a.* 1.

Line, Lina, 1. Snöre, 4.

Lining, Foder, 5.

Link, Länk, 2.

Lint, Linskaf, *s. n.*

Lion, Lejon, 5.

Lip, Läpp, 2.

Liquid, Flytande, *ad.*

List, Lista, 1.

Listen, Lyssna, *a.* 1.

Little, Liten, *ad.*

Live, Lefva, *a.* 2.

Liver, Lefver, 2.

Load, Last, 3. Lass, 5.

Loadstone, Magnet, 3.

Lobster, Hummer, 2.

Lock, Lås, 5. Låsa, *a.* 3.

Lodging, Boningsrum, 5.

Lofty, Hög, Stolt, *ad.*

Loin, Länd, 3.

Look, Blick, 2. Se, *i.* 3.

Loose, Lös, *ad.*

Loss, Förlust, 3.

Loud, Gäll, Högljudd, *ad.*

Love, Kärlek, *s. c.*

Lovely, Täck, Älskvärd, *ad.*

Lover, { Älskare 5.
{ Älskarinna, 1.

Louse, Lus, *pl.* Löss.

Low, Låg, *ad.*

Lump, Massa, 1. Stycke, 4.

Luncheon, Litselmiddag, *s. c.*

Lungs, Lungor, *sing.* Lunga.

Lustre, Glans, *s. c.* Sken, 5.

Luxury, Yppighet, *s. o.*

Lyre, Lyra, 1.

Mad, Galen, *ad.*

Maid, Piga, 1. Jungfru, 3.

Mail, Post, 3. Postväska, 1.

Make, Göra, *a.* 2.

Male, Hanne, 2.

Malt, Malt, *s. n.*

Man, Man, *pl.* Män.

Man, Menniska, 1.

Man of War, Örlogs-skepp.

Mane, Man, 2.

Manly, Manlig, *ad.*

Manner, Sed, 3. Sätt, 5.

Manure, Gödsel, *s. c.*

Many, Många, *ad.*

Map, Karta, 1. Sjökort, 5.

Marble, Marmor, *s. c.*

Mark, Märke, 4.

Market, Marknad, Pris, 3.

Marriage, Giftermål, 5.

Marrow, Merg, *s. c.*

Marsh, Kärr, 5. Moras, 3.

Mason, Murmästare, 5.

Mat, Matta, 1.

Match, Parti, 3.

Matches, Svafvelstickor, 1.

Mate, Styrman.

Mathematics, Matematik, *s. c.*

Matrimony, Ägtenskap, 3.

Matter, Ämne, 4. Materie, 3.

Mature, Mogen, *ad.*

Maxim, Grundsats. 3.

Meadow, Äng, 2.

Meal, Mål, 5. Måltid. 3.

Mean, Låg, Ringa, *ad.*

Means, Medel, 5.

Mean, Mena, *a.* 1.

Measles, Messling, *s. c.*

Measure, Mått, 5.

Meat, Kött, *s. n.* Kötträtt. 3.

Mediator, Medlare, 5.

Medium, Medelväg, *s. c.*

Meet, Möta, *a.* 3. Råka, *a.* 1. 3.

Member, Lem, 2. Ledamot, 3.

Memory, Minne, 4.

Mend, Laga, Ändra, *a.* 1.

Mention, Omtala, *a.* 1. 3.

Mercy, Nåd, *s. e.*

Merit, Förtjenst, 3. Förtjena.

Merry, Lustig, Glad, *ad.*

Message, Budskap, 5.

Meteor, Luft-tecken, 5.

Midwife, Jodgumma, 1.

Mile, Mil, 2.

Milk, Mjölk, *s. c.*

Mill, Qvarn, 2.

Mind, Sinne, 4. Märka, *a.* 3.

Mine, Grufva, 1.

Minor, Omyndig, *ad.*

Mischief, Ofog, 5. Skada, 1.

Misery, Elände, 4.

Misfortune, Olycka, 1.

Mislead, Förleda, *a.* 2.

Miss, Jungfru, Mamsell, 3.

Mistake, Misstag, 5. Misstaga,

Mistress, Fru, Matmor, 2. [*i.* 2.

Misty, Töcknig, *ad.*

Mix, Blanda, *a.* 1.

Mock, Gäcka, *a.* 1.

Modest, Sedig, Blygsam, *ad.*

Moist, Fuktig.

Moment, Vigt, *s. c.* Ögonblick,

Money, Penningar, *p.* [5.

Month, Månad, 3.

Moon, Måne, 2.

Morning, Morgon, 2.

Mortar, Mortel, 2.

Moss, Laf, 2. Mossa, 1.

Mother, Moder, 2.

Motion, Rörelse, 3. Stolgång,

Move, Röra, *a.* 2. Flytta. [2.

Mould, Form, 2. Forma, *a.* 1.

Mountain, Berg, 5.

Mouth, Mun, 2.

Mud, Gyttja, Dy, *s. c.*

Multitude, Myckenhet, 3.

Murder, Mord, 5.

Muscle, Muskel, 2.

Mustard, Senap, *s. c.*

Muster, Mönstra, *a.* 1.

Mutiny, Myteri, 3.

Mutton, Fårkött, *s. n.*

Mystery, Hemlighet, 3.

Nail, Nagel, Spik, 2.

Naked, Naken, *ad.*

Name, Namn, 5.

Namely, Nemligen.

Nap, Lur, *s. c.* Lura, Slumra.

Narrow, Trång, Smal, *ad.*

Nasty, Oren, Ful, *ad.*

Native, Inföding, 2.

Naval Engagement, *Sjöslag.*

Navel, Nafle, 2.

Naughty, Elak, *ad.*

Navy, Krigs-Flotta, 1.

Near, Nära, Närbelägen, *ad.*

Neat, Nätt, Täck, *ad.*

Necessity, Nödvändighet, 3.

Neck, Huls, s.

Neckcloth, Halsduk, 2.

Need, Nöd, s. c.

Needle, Synål, 2.

Needs, Nödvändigt.

Neglect, Försumma, a. 1.

Neighbour, Granne, 2. Nabo, [3.

Nest, Näste, Bo, 4.

Never, Aldrig.

New, Ny, Färsk, ad.

News, Nytt, Nyhet, 3.

Next, Näst.

Nice, Vacker, Läcker, ad.

Nickname, Öknamn, 5.

Night, Natt, pl. Nätter.

Nimble, Vig, Snabb, ad.

Nod, Nick, 2. Nicka, a. 1.

Noise, Buller, 5.

Noon, Middagstid.

Nose, Näsa, 1.

Nothing, Ingenting.

Notion, Begrepp, 5. Tanke.

Novelty, Nyhet, 3.

Nourish, Föda, Nära, a. 2.

Now, Nu.

Number, Tal, Antal, 5.

Numberless, Otalig, ad.

Nurse, Sköterska, 1.

Wet-Nurse, Amma, 1.

Nutmeg, Muskott, 5.

Nutriment, Föda, s. e.

Oak, Ek, 2.

Oar, Åra, 1.

Obedient, Lydig, ad.

Obey, Lyda, a. 2.

Object, Föremål, 5.

Obligation, Förbindelse, 3.

Oblong, Aflång, ad.

Obstacle, Hinder, Motstånd.

Obstinate, Envis, ad.

Obstruction, Förstoppning.

Obtain, Erhålla, i. 2.

Obvious, Tydlig, ad.

Occasion, Tilfälle, 4.

Occupy, Innehafva.

Occur, Förekomma, i. 4.

Odd, Udda, Sällsam, ad.

Offence, Skada, 1. Förtret, 3.

Offend, Förtörna, a. 1.

Office, Tjenst, 3. Kontor, 5.

Post-Office, Post-Kontor, 5.

Often, Ofta.

Oil, Olja, 1.

Ointment, Smörjelse, 3.

Oister, Ostra, pl. Ostron, ce

Old, Gammal, ad.

Omit, Underlåta, i. 2.

Once, Engång, Fordom.

Only, Endast, Allenast.

Open, Öppen, ad.

Opiate, Sömndryck, 3.

Oppress,

Oppress, Förtrycka, *a.* 3.

Opulent, Rik, Förmögen, *ad.*

Order, Ordning, 2. Påbud, 5.

Ore, Malm, 3.

Oriental, Österländsk, *ad.*

Origin, Ursprung, 5.

Ornament, Prydnad, 3.

Ostentation, Skryt, 5.

Ostler, Hållkarl, Stalldräng, 2.

Otherwise, Annars.

Oven, Ugn, 2.

Over, Öfver.

Out, Ut.

Outlet, Utgång, 2.

Outside, Utsida, 1.

Outwork, Utanverk, 5.

Owe, Vara skyldig.

Owl, Uggla, 1.

Own, Egen, *ad.*

Owner, Ägare, 5.

Ox, Oxe, 2.

Pace, Gång, *s. c.* Steg, 5.

Pack, Packa, *a.* 1.

Padlock, Utanlås, Hänglås, 5.

Page, Sida (i en bok) 1.

Pail, Ämbar, 5.

Pain, Möda, Plåga, 1.

Paint, Färg, 3. Smink, 5.

Paint, Måla, *a.* 1.

Pair, Par, 5.

Palate, Gom, 2.

Pale, Blek, *ad.*

Palpable, Handgriplig, *ad.*

Pamphlet, Ströskrift, 3.

Pan, Panna, 1.

Pane, Fönster-ruta, 1.

Paper, Papper, 5.

Parcel, Bunt, 2. Knyte, 4.

Parchment, Pergament, 5.

Parish, Socken, 2.

Parsley, Persilja, *s. c.*

Parsnip, Palsternacka, 1.

Part, Del, 2. Lott, 3.

Part, Dela, *a.* 1. Skilja, *a.* 2.

Partly, Dels.

Pass, Passera, *a.* 1.

Path, Stig, Väg, 2.

Patience, Tålamod, *s. c.*

Paw, Ram, Tass, 2.

Pawn, Pant, 3.

Pay, Betalning, 2.

Pay, Betala, *a.* 3.

Pea, Ärt, 3.

Peace, Fred, 3. Lugn, *s. n.*

Pear, Päron, 5.

Pearch, Aborre, 2.

Peasant, Bonde, *pl.* Bönder.

Peek, Spets, Pik, 2.

Peel, Skal, 5.

Pen, Penna, 1.

Penetrate, Genomtränga, *a.* 2.

9

Pensive, Tankfull, *ad.*

People, Folk, 5.

Pepper, Peppar, *s. c.*

Perfect, Fullkomlig, *ad.*

Perform, Uträtta, *a.* 1.

Perhaps, Kanske.

Peril, Fara, 1.

Perish, Förgås, *d. i.*

Perjury, Mened, 3.

Permit, Tillåta, *i.* 2.

Perpetual, Beständig, *ad.*

Perry, Päron-vin.

Personal, Personlig, *ad.*

Persuade, Öfvertala, *a.* 1. 3.

Pert, Näsvis, *ad.*

Peruse, Genomläsa, *a.* 3.

Pestle, Mortel-stöt, 2.

Pew, Bänk (i kyrkan), 2.

Phrase, Talesätt, 5.

Pick, Plocka, Hacka, *a.* 1.

Pickle, Lake, *s. o.*

Picklock, Dyrk, 2.

Pickpocket, Ficktjuf, 2.

Picture, Målning, 2.

Piece, Stycke, 4.

Piety, Gudsfruktan, *s. o.*

Pig, Gris, Galt, 2.

Pigeon, Dufva, 1.

Pike, Gädda (a fish) 1. Pik, 2.

Pill, Piller, 5.

Pillow, Kudde, 2.

Pilot, Lots, 2.

Pin, Knappnål, 2.

Pincers, Hoftång, 3.

Pinch, Nypa, *a.* 3.

Pine, Gran, 2.

Pious, Gudfruktig, *ad.*

Pipe, Pipa, 1.

Pirate, Sjöröfvare, 5.

Pit, Grop, 2. Parterr, 3.

Pitch, Beck, *s. n.* Höjd, 3.

Pitcher, Stenkrus, 5. Kruka

Pity, Medlidande, *s. n.*

Place, Plats, 3. Ställa, *a.* 2

Plain, Slät, *ad.* Slätt, 3.

Plain, Släta, Jemna, *a.* 1.

Plank, Planka, 1.

Plant, Plantera, *a.* 1.

Plate, Tallrik, 2. Silfverkärl

Play, Spel, 5. Komedi, 3.

Pleasant, Behaglig, *ad.*

Please, Behaga, *a.* 1.

If you please, Om ni behagar

Pleasure, Nöje, 4.   [*s. o*

Pledge, Pant, 3. Försäkran

Plenty, Ymnighet, *s. o.*

Plow, Plog, 2.

Plum, Plommon, 5.

Point, Udd, Spets, 2.

Poison, Förgift, *s. n.*

Poker, Eldgaffel, 2.

Polite, Höflig, *ad.*

Pomatum, Pomada, 1.

Pond, Dam, 2.

Poop, Bakstam, 2.

Poor, Fattig, ad.

Pope, Påfve, 2.

Pork, Svinkött, s. n.

Port, Hamn, 2. Portvin.

Porter, Bärare, 5.

Postage, Postpenningar, p.

Postpone, Eftersätta, i. 4.

Pot, Potta, 1. Stop, 5.

Potatoes, Potäter, pl. Potates.

Poultry, Fjäderfä, s. n. Höns.

Pound. Mark, 3.

Pour, Gjuta, c. 2. Strömma.

Powder, Puder, s. n. Pulver, 5.

Power, Magt, 3. Välde, 3.

Practice, Öfning, 2.

Prate, Prata, a. 1.

Pray, Bedja, i. 4.

Prayer, Bön, 3.

Prayerbook, Psalmbok, 3.

Preach, Predika, a. 1.

Precipice, Brant, 3. Brådjup.

Preface, Företal, 5.   [5.

Prefer, Föredraga, i. 2.

Preferment, Befordran, s. c.

Prepare, Laga (a. 1.) til.

Present, Skänk, 3.

Present, Närvarande, ad.

Presently, Strax.

Preserves, Syltsaker, p.

Press, Bokpress, 2.   [1.

Press, Trycka, a. 3. Pressa, a.

Presume, Förmoda, a. 1.

Pretence, Förevändning, 2.

Pretend, Påstå, i. 3.

Pretension, Anspråk, 5.

Prevalent, Rådande, ad.

Prevent, Förekomma, i. 4.

Price, Pris, 5. Värde, 4.

Pride, Högmod, s. n.

Prince, Prins, Furste, 2.

Princess, Prinsessa, 1.

Print, Tryck, Kopparstick, 5.

Prison, Fängelse, 3.

Privy, Privet, 5.

Prize, Pris, 3. Byte, s. n.

Procure, Förskaffa, a. 1.

Produce, Frambringa, i. 4.

Produce, Afkastning, s. c.

Progress, Framsteg, 5.

Promise, Löfte, 4. Lofva, a. 1.

Promote, Befordra, a. 1.

Proof, Prof, Bevis, 5.

Property, Egendom, s. c. Art.

Propose, Föreslå, i. 3.   [3.

Propriety, Tilbörlighet, s. c.

Prosperity, Välgång, s. c.

Protection, Beskydd, 5.

Proud, Högfärdig, Stolt, ad.

Provoke, Reta, Förarga, a. 1.

Proxy, Fullmägtig.

Prunes, Sviskon, 5.

Public, Allmän, *ad*.

Publican, Krögare, 5.

Puff, Skryt, *s. n.* Snutt, 2.

Pull, Draga, *i.* 2. Rycka, *a.* 3.

Pulpit, Predikstol, 2.

Pump, Pump, 2. Pumpa, *a.* 1.

Punish, Straffa, *a.* 1.

Purchase, Köpa, *a.* 3.

Pure, Pur, Ren, *ad*.

Purpose, Ändamål, 5.

Purse, Pung, 2.

Purser, Skepps-Skrifvare, 5.

Pursue, Fullfölja, *a.* 2.

Push, Stöt, 2. Stöta, *a.* 3.

Put, Sätta, *i.* 4. Ställa, *a.* 2.

Putrid, Rutten, *ad*.

Puzzle, Bryderi, 3.

Qualified, Skicklig, *ad*.

Quality, Egenskap, 3. Art, 3.

Quantity, Myckenhet, *s. c.*

Quarrel, Träta, 1. Gräl, 5.

Quarter, Fjerndel, 2. Pardon.

Quay, Kaj, 2. Stenbrygga, 1.

Queen, Drottning, 2.

Quench, Släcka, *a.* 3.

Question, Fråga, 1.

Quick, Lefvande, *ad*.

Quiet Stilla, *ad*.

Quill, Penna, 1. (Oskuren).

Quilt, Sängtäcke, 4.

Quire, Bok, (papper) 3.

Quit, Lemna, *a.* 1.

Quiver, Darra, *a.* 1.

Rabbet, Kanin, 3.

Race, Slägte, 4. Lopp, 5.

Radish, Rädisa, 1.

Black Radish, Rättika, 1.

Rag, Trasa, 1.

Rage, Rasa, *a.* 1. Raseri, 3.

Rail, Ledstång, 3.

Rain, Regn, *s. c.*

Rainbow, Regnbåge, 2.

Rainy, Regnig, *ad*.

Rank, Rang, *s. c.* Rad, 3.

Ransom, Lösepenning, 2.

Rapid, Hastig, *ad*.

Rapture, Förtjusning, *s. c.*

Rascal, Skurk, 2.

Rash, Oförvägen, *ad*.

Rate, Värdera, *a.* 1.

Ratify, Stadfästa, *a.* 1.

Ravage, Plundra, *a.* 1.

Rave, Yra, Rasa, *a.* 1.

Raw, Rå, *ad*.

Ray, Stråle, 2.

Razor, Rakknif, 2.

Reach, Räcka, *a.* 3.

Read, Läsa, *a.* 3.

Ready, Färdig, *ad.*

Reason, Förnuft, *s. n.*

Receipt, Recept, Qvittens, 3.

Receive, Emottaga, *i.* 2.

Recently, Nyligen.

Reckon, Räkna, *a.* 1.

Reckoning, Räkning, 2.

Recollect, Komma ihåg.

Recovery, Återfående, *s. n.*

Recreation, Muntring, *s. c.*

Rectify, Rätta, *a.* 1.

Red, Röd, *ad.*

Redeemer, Återlösare, 5.

Redemption, Återlösning, 2.

Redress, Ändring, 2.

Reef, Ref, 5.

Refer, Hänvisa, *a.* 3.

Refresh, Förfriska, *a.* 1.

Refreshment, Förfriskning, 2.

Refuge, Tilflykt, 3.

Refuse, Vägra, *a.* 1.

Regard, Aktning, *s. c.*

Reject, Förkasta, *a.* 1.

Reign, Regering, 2.

Rein, Töm, 2.

Relate, Berätta, *a.* 1.

Relation, Berättelse, 3.

Relief, Hjelp, *s. c.*

Relish, Smak, *s. c.* Tycka om.

Rely, Lita på, *i.* 2.

Remain, Blifva qvar, (p. 83).

Remark, Anmärka, *a.* 3.

Remedy, Bot, *s. c.*

Remember, Påminna, *a.* 3.

Remote, Aflägsen, *ad.*

Remove, Flytta, *a.* 1.

Renew, Förnya, *a.* 1.

Repair, Laga, Förbättra, *a.* 1.

Repeat, Uprepa, *a.* 1.

Repent, Ångra, *a.* 1.

Report, Rygte, 4. Berätta, *a.* 1.

Repose, Hvila, *s. c.*

Represent, Föreställa, *a.* 2.

Reproach, Förebråelse.

Request, Begära, Begäran, *s. c.*

Rescue, Rädda, Frälsa, *a.* 1.

Resemble, Likna, *a.* 1.

Reside, Vistas, *d.* 1.

Resign, Afträda, *a.* 2.

Resist, Emotstå, *i.* 3.

Resolve, Besluta, *i.* 2.

Rest, Hvila, Sömn, *s. o.*

Restore, Återställa, *a.* 2.

Retail, Dela, Minutera, *a.* 1.

Retain, Behålla, *i.* 2.

Return, Återvända, *a.* 2.

Revelation, Uppenbarelse, 3.

Revenge, Hämnd, Hämnas, *d.*

Review, Mönstring, 2. [1.

Revoke, Återkalla, *a.* 1.

Reward, Belöning, 2.

Rib, Refben, 3.

Rice, Risgryn, 5.

Rich, Rik, *ad.*

Rid, Fri, Befriad, *ad.*

Ride, Åka, *a.* 3. Rida, *i.* 2.

Rie, Råg, *s. c.*

Rig, Tackla, *a.* 1.

Right, Rigtig, Rätt, *ad.*

Right, Rättighet, 3.

Right hand, Höger hand.

Ring, Ring, Cirkel, 2.

Ripe, Mogen, *ad.*

Rise, Upkomst, *s. c.* Stå up.

River, Flod, 3, Elf, 2.

Road, Väg, 2. Redd, *s. c.*

Roast, Steka, *a.* 3.

Rob, Röfva, *a.* 1.

Rock, Klippa, 1.

Rod, Spö, 4. Ris, 5.

Rogue, Skälm, 2.

Roof, Tak, 5.

Room, Rum, 5. Kammare, 5.

Root, Rot, *pl.* Rötter.

Rope, Tåg, Rep, 5.

Rough, Ojemn, Skroflig, *ad.*

Round, Rund, *ad.*

Row, Rad, 3. Ro, *a.* 2.

Royal, Kunglig, *ad.*

Rub, Gnida, *i.* 2.

Rudder, Roder, 5.

Rude, Grof, Ohöflig, *ad.*

Rue, Ångra, Rua, *a.* 1.

Rug, Rya, 1.

Ruin, Förderf, 5. Förderfva

Rule, Ordning, 2. Bruk, 5.

Rum, Rom, *s. c.*

Rumour, Rygte, 4.

Run, Löpa, *a.* 3. Springa, *i.* 1

Rust, Rost, Härsknad, *s. c.*

Sabre, Sabel, 2.

Sack, Säck, 2.

Saddle, Sadel, 2.

Safe, Säker, Trygg, *ad.*

Sail, Segel, 5. Segla, *a.* 1.

Sailor, Sjöman, *pl.* Sjömän.

Salmon, Lax, 2.

Salt, Salt, *s. n.*

Salutation, Helsning, 2.

Salute, Helsa, *a.* 1.

Salvation, Frälsning, *s. c.*

Sample, Prof, 5.

Sand, Sand, *s. c.*

Sands, Sandbankar, 2. *pl.*

Sauce, Sås, 3.

Saucy, Näsvis, *ad.*

Saviour, Frälsare, 5.

Saw, Såg, 2.

Say, Säga, *impf.* Sade.

Scale, Skala, 1. Måttstock,

Scales, Vågskål, 2.

Scanty, Knapp, Dålig, *ad.*

Scar, Ärr, 5. Skråma, 1.

Scarce, Knappt.

Scarf, Slöja, 1. Band, 5.

Scate, Skridsko, 3.

Scavenger, Gatsopare, 5.

Scheme, Plan, Förslag, 5.

School, Skole, 2.

Schoolfellow, Skolkamrat, 3.

Science, Vetenskap, 3.

Scissors, Sax, 2.

Scold, Banna, *a.* 1. Träta, *a.* 3.

Score, Tjog, 5.

Scorn, Förakt, *s. n.* Förakta, *a.*

Scrape, Skrapa, *a.* 1. [1.

Scratch, Rifva, *i.* 2. Klå, *a.* 2.

Scream, Skrika, *i.* 2. Skria, *a.*

Screen, Skärm, 2. [1.

Screw, Skruf, 2. Skrufva, *a.* 1.

Scripture, Skrift, 3. Bibel, 2.

Scurvy, Skörbjugg, *s. c.*

Sea, Haf, 5. Sjö, 2.

Seafaring, Sjöfarande, *ad.*

Seasick, Sjösjuk, *ad.*

Seal, Sigill, 5. Försegla, *a.* 1.

Seam, Söm, 2. Sömma, *a.* 1.

Search, Spaning, 2. Spana, *a.* 1.

Season, Årstid, 3. Kryddning.

Seat, Säte, 4.

Secret, Hemlig, Hemlighet.

Secure, Säker, Trygg, *ad.*

Sediment, Grummel, Drägg.

Seduce, Förföra, Förleda, *a.* 2.

See, Se, *i.* 3.

Seed, Frö, 4.

Seek, Söka, *a.* 3.

Seem, Synas, Tyckas, *d.* 3.

Seize, Gripa, *i.* 2. Confiskera.

Seldom, Sällan.

Select, Utvald, *ad.*

Sell, Sälja, *a.* 2.

Se'nnight, Åtta dar.

Sense, Förstånd, *s. n.* Sinne, 4.

Sentence, Dom, Mening, 2.

Separate, Särskilt, *ad.*

Serious, Allvarsam, *ad.*

Sermon, Predikan, *s. c.*

Serpent, Orm, 2.

Servant, Tjenare, 5. Dräng, 2.

Set, Sätta, *i.* 4. Gå ned.

The Sun sets, Solen går ned.

Settle, Stadga, Betala, *a.* 1. 3.

Sew, Sy, *a.* 2. Sömma, *a.* 1.

Sex, Kön, 5.

Shabby, Dålig, Usel, *ad.*

Shade, Skugga, 1.

Shake, Skaka, Darra, *a.* 1.

Shame, Skam, *s. c.*

Shape, Skapnad, 3.

Share, Del, 2. Lott, 3.

Shark, Haj, 2.

Sharp, Skarp, Hvass, *ad.*

Sharper, Bedragare, 5.

Shave, Raka, *a.* 1.

Sheath, Skida, 1.

Shed, Utgjuta, *impf.* Utgöt.

Sheep, Får, 5. Tacka, 1.

Sheet, Lakan, *s. n.* Ark, 5.

Shelter, Skjul, Försvar, 5.

Shew, Visa, *a.* 1. 3.

Shield, Sköld, 2.

Shift, Utväg, Särk, 2.

Shine, Skina, *i.* 1. Lysa, *a.* 3.

Ship, Skepp, Fartyg, 5.

Shirt, Skjorta, 1.

Shoar, Strand, *pl.* Stränder.

Shock, Stöta, *a.* 3.

Shoe, Sko, 3. Sko, *a.* 2.

Shoot, Skjuta, *i.* 2.

Shop, Bod, 2. Verkstad, 3.

Short, Kort, *ad.*

Shoulder, Skuldra, 1. Bog, 2.

Shrove-tide, Fastlag, *s. c.*

Shudder, Rysa, *a.* 3.

Shun, Sky, Undfly, *a.* 2.

Sheet, Stänga, *a.* 2.

Shy, Skygg, Blyg, *ad.*

Sick, Qvalmig, Sjuk, *ad.*

Side, Sida, 1.

Sieve, Sikt, 5.

Sign, Tecken, 5. Teckna, *a.* 1.

Silence, Tystnad, *s. c.*

Silk, Silke, 4. Siden, 5.

Silver, Silfver, *s. n.*

Sin, Synd, 3. Synda, *a.* 1.

Since, Sedan.

Sincere, Redlig, *ad.*

Sinew, Sena, 1.

Sing, Sjunga, *i.* 4.

Sink, Sjunka, *i.* 4. Sänka, *a.* 3.

Sip, Läppja, Smutta, *a.* 1.

Sister, Syster, 2.

Sit, Sitta, *i.* 4.

Situation, Belägenhet, 3.

Size, Storlek, 2.

Sketch, Utkast, 5,

Skill, Skicklighet, 3. Förstånd.

Skin, Skinn, 5. Hud, 2.

Sky, Sky, 2. Luft, *s. c.*

Sledge, Släde, 2.

Sleep, Sömn, *s. c.* Sofva, *i.* 2.

Sleepy, Sömnig, Tung, *ad.*

Sleeve, Arm, 2.

Slice, Skifva, 1.

Slide, Slinta, Skrilla, *a.* 1.

Slight, Ringa, Tunn, *ad.*

Slop, Paska, *a.* 1. Väta, *a.* 3.

Slope, Slutta, *a.* 1.

Slow, Trög, Sen, *ad.*

Slumber, Slumra, *a.* 1.

Sly, Slug, Illparig, *ad.*

Small, Liten, *def.* Lilla.

Smart, Smärta, Sveda, *s. c.*

Smell, Lukt, *s. c.* Lukta, *a.* 1.

Smile, Le, Småle, *i.* 3.

Smith, Smed, 3.

Smoak, Rök, *s. c.* Röka, *a.* 3.

Smooth, Slät, Jemn, *ad.*

Snare, Snara, 1. Nät, 5.

Snatch, Snappa, *a.* 1.

Sneeze, Nysa, *a.* 3.

Snore, Snarka, *a.* 1.

Snow, Snö, *s. c.*

Snuff, Snus, *s. n.* Snyta, *i.* 2.

Soap, Såpa, Tvål, *s. c.*

Sober, Nykter, Ärbar, *ad.*

Soft, Mjuk, Öm, *ad.*

Soil, Jordmån, *s. c.*

Soldier, Soldat, 3.

Some-Body, Någon, *ad.*

Sometimes, Stundom.

Son, Son, *pl.* Söner.

Song, Sång, 3. *Soon, Snart.*

Sooth, Lindra, Stilla, *a.* 2.

Sore, Öm, Svidsam, *ad.*

Sorrow, Sorg, 3. Sörja, *a.* 2.

Sorry, Sorgsen, Ledsen, *ad.*

Soul, Själ, 2.

Sound, Sund, Frisk, *ad.*

Sound, Ljud, 5. Ljuda, *a.* 2.

Sound, Sund, 5.

Sour, Sur, Tvär, *ad.*

Sow, Så, *a.* 2. Utkasta, *a.* 1.

Space, Rymd, 3. Rum, 5.

Spade, Spade, 2.

Spare, Spara, *a.* 2.

Spark, Gnista, 1.

Sparrow, Sparf, 2.

Speak, Tala, *a.* 1. 3.

Species, Slag, 5. Art, 3.

Specimen, Prof, 5.

Spectacles, Glasögon, *p.*

Speech, Mål, Tal, 3.

Speed, Hast, *s. c.* Hasta, *a.* 1.

Spell, Stafva, *a.* 1.

Spencer, Utantröja, 1.

Spice, Krydda, 1. Speceri, 3.

Spire, Spira, 1.

Spirit, Ande, 2. Mod, *s. n.*

Splendor, Glans, Ståt, *s. c.*

Split, Klyfva, *i.* 2. Spräcka, *a.* 3.

Spoil, Förderfva, *a.* 1. Skäm-[ma.

Spoon, Sked, 2.

Sport, Lek, 2. Jagt, *s. c.*

Spot, Fläck, 2. Ställe, 4.

Spout, Pip, 2.

Spread, Sprida, Breda, *a.* 2.

Spring, Källa, 1. Vår, 2.

Spring-tide, Hafs-flöde, 4.

Sprinkle. Stänka, *a.* 3.

Sprucebeer, Tallstruntöl, *s. n.*

Spunge, Svamp, 2.

Spur, Sporre, 2.

Spy, Spion, 3. Spionera, *a.* 1.

Square, Fyrkantig, *ad.* Torg, 5.

Squeeze, Krama, Krysta, *a.* 1.

Stable, Stall, 5.

Stage, Theater, Gästgifveri, 3.

Stair, Trappa, 1.

Upstairs, Ofvanpå.

Downstairs, Nere.

Stalk, Stjelk, 2.

Stamp, Stämpel, 2. Stämpla, 1.

Star, Stjerna, 1.

Starch, Stärkelse, s. c.

Start, Hoppa, a. 1. Afresa, 3.

Starve, Svälta, i. 1. Frysa, i. 2.

State, Tilstånd, 5.

States, Ständer, p.

Statue, Stod, Staty, 3.

Staves, Stäfver, p.

Stay, Vänta, a. 1. Dröja, a. 2.

Stays, Snörlif, 5.

Steady, Stadig, Fast, ad.

Steal, Stjäla, impf. Stal.

Steam, Änga, 1. Dunst, 3.

Steam-engine, Eld och luft

Steel, Stål, s. n. [machin 3.

Steep, Brant, ad.

Steer, Styra, a. 2.

Step, Steg, Spår, 5.

Stern, Bakstam, 2. Tver, ad.

Stew, Stufva, a. 1.

Stick, Käpp, 2. Fastna, a. 1.

Stiff, Styf, Stel, ad.

Stile, Stil, Pragt, s. c.

Still, Stilla, ad. Ännu.

Sting, Sting, 5. Stinga, i. 1.

Stir, Upröra, a. 2.

Stirrup, Stegbygel, 2.

Stich, Sticka, i. 1. Lappa, a. 1.

Stock, Förråd, 5. Fond, 3.

Stomach, Mage, 2. Aptit, s. a.

Stone, Sten, Kärne.

Stoop, Stupa, Luta, a. 1.

Stop, Hejda, Stadna, a. 1.

Store, Vara, 1. Förråd, 5.

Storm, Storm 2. Bestorma, a. 1.

Story, Historie, 3. Våning, 2.

Stout, Styf, Stor, Stark, ad.

Strain, Sila, Krama, a. 1.

Straight, Rät, Rak, ad. Rätt.

Strange, Underlig, ad.

Stranger, Främling, 2.

Strap, Stroppa, 1.

Stream, Ström, 2.

Street, Gata, 1.

Strength, Styrka, s. c.

Stretch, Sträcka, a. 3.

Strike, Slå, i. 3. Bulta, a. 1.

String, Sträng, 2. Band, 5.

Shoe String, Sko-band.

Strip, Beröfva, a. 1. Afkläda.

Strong, Stark, Dugtig, ad.

Struggle, Bemödande, Strid.

Stupid, Dum, Dåragtig, ad.

Subdue, Underkufva, a. 1.

Subject, Ämne, 4. Undersåte.

Submit, Underkasta, a. 1.

Subsidy, Bevillning, 2.

Subsist, Lefva, *a.* 2. Bestå, *i.* 3.

Suburbs, Förstad, 3.

Succeed, Efterträda, Lyckas.

Success, Framgång, Lycka.

Succour, Hjelp, *s. c.* Hjelpa, *a.* 3.

Suck, Suga, *i.* 2. Di, *a.* 2.

Sue, Bedja, *i.* 4. Ansöka, *a.* 3.

Suffer, Lida, *i.* 2. Tåla, *a.* 3.

Sufficient, Tilräcklig, *ad.*

Sugar, Socker, *s. n.*

Summer, Sommar, 2.

Sun, Sol, 2. Sunday, Söndag, 2.

Superficial, Ytlig, *ad.*

Sure, Säker, Viss, *ad.*

Surgeon, Fältskär, 2.

Surround, Omgifva.

Survey, Syna, Besigtiga, *a.* 1.

Suspect, Misstänka, *a.* 3.

Swallow, Svala, 1. Svälja, *a.* 2.

Sweat, Svett, *s. c.* Svettas, *d.* 1.

Sweep, Sopa, *a.* 1. Sweet, Söt.

Swift, Snabb, Snar, *ad.*

Swim, Simma, *i.* 1.

Swing, Gunga, 1. Gunga, *a.* 1.

Swoon, Svimning, 2. Svimma.

Sword, Värja, 1. Svärd, 5.

Symptom, Tecken, 5. Anstöt.

Syrup, Socker-Sirap, *s. c.*

Table, Bord, 5.

Tail, Svans, Stjert, 2.

Take, Taga, *i.* 2. Fatta, *a.* 1.

Talk, Tal, 5. Tala, *a.* 1. 3.

Tall, Lång, Reslig, *ad.*

Tallow, Talg, *s. c.*

Tame, Tam, Spak, *ad.*

Tan, Garfva, *a.* 1.

Tankard, Kanna, Stånka, 1.

Tar, Tjära, *s. c.* Matros, 3.

Tarry, Dröja, *a.* 2.

Tart, Tärta, 1.

Task, Syssla, 1.

Taste, Smak, *s. c.* Smaka, *a.* 1.

Tavern, Värdshus, Källare, 5.

Taylor, Skräddare, 5.

Tea, Té, 3.

Teach, Lära, *a.* 2. Undervisa.

Tear, Tår, 2.

Teaze, Plåga, *a.* 1. Bry, *a.* 2.

Telescope, Kikare, 5.

Tell, Berätta, *a.* 1. Säga, 4.

Temper, Lynne, 4.

Tenant, Åbo, 3.

Tend, Syfta (på) *a.* 1.

Tender, Press-skepp, 5.

Tent, Tält, 5.

Terrible, Förskräcklig, *ad.*

Test, Prof, Försök, 5.

Testify, Intyga, *a.* 1.

Thank, Tacka, *a.* 1.

Thaw, Tö, *s. n.* Töa, *a.* 1.

Thick, Tjock, *ad.*

Thief, 2. Tjuf. 2,

Thigh, Lår, 5.

Thimble, Fingerbor, 2.

Thing, Ting, 5, Sak, 3.

Thin, Tunn, *ad.*

Think, Tänka, *a.* 3.

Thirst, Törst, *s. c.*

Thirsty, Törstig, *ad.*

Thistle, Tistel, 2.

Thorn, Törne, 4.

Thought, Tanke, 2. Upsåt, 5.

Thrash, Tröska, *a.* 1.

Thread, Tråd, 2. Träda, *a.* 2.

Threaten, Hota, *a.* 1.

Thrive, Trifvas, *d.* 2.

Throat, Hals, Strupe, 2.

Throw, Kast, 5. Kasta, *a.* 1.

Thumb, Tumme, 2.

Thunder, Thordön, *s. n.* Åska.

Tick, Bolstervar, 5.

Ticket, Sedel, 2. Biljett, 3.

Tide, Tid, *s. c.* (Ebb och Flod).

Tie, Knut, 2. Knyta, *i.* 2.

Tight, Tät, Spänd, *ad.*

Tile, Tak-Tegel, 5.

Till, Odla, Upbruka, *a.* 1.

Time, Tid, 3.   [3.

Tin, Tenn, *s. n.* Förtenna, *a.* 1.

Tinder, Fnöske, Sköre, *s. n.*

Tinder-box, Skör-ask, 2.

Tire, Trötta, Tröttna, *a.* 1.

Tiresome, Tröttsam, Tråkig.

Toast, Skål, 2.

Toe, Tå, 3.

Toil, Arbete, 4. Arbeta, *a.* 1.

Tolerable, Dräglig, *ad.*

Tomb, Graf, 2. Grift, 3.

Tongs, Tång, *pl.* Tänger.

Tool, Verktyg, Redskap, 5.

Tooth, Tand, *pl.* Tänder, 3.

Torch, Fackla, 1.

Torment, Plåga, 1. Plåga, *a.* 1.

Tortoise, Sköldpadda, 1.

Touch, Känsel, *s. c.* Röra, 2.

Tow, Tåg, 5. Boxera, *a.* 1.

Towards, Emot, Åt. Til.

Tower, Kastell, 5. Fäste, 4.

Town, Stad, *pl.* Städer, 3.

Trace, Upspana, *a.* 1.

Trade, Handtverk, Födkrok.

Train, Släp, 5. Följe, 4.

Train, Upamma, *a.* 1.

Train-oil, Tran, *s. c.*

Transfer, Öfverföra, *a.* 2.

Translate, Öfversätta, *i.* 4.

Transmit, Öfversända, *a.* 2.

Trap, Fälla, 1.

Travel, Resa, 1. Resa, *a.* 3.

Traveller, Resande, *ad.*

Treacle, Sirap, (brun) *s. c.*

Treason, Förräderi, 3.

Treasure, Skatt, 3.

Treat, Traktera, Afhandla, *a.*   Unaccountable, Obegriplig.

Treatise, Afhandling, 2. [1. Unaffected, Otvungen *ad.*

Treaty, Traktat, 3.   Unanimous, Enhällig, *ad.*

Tree, Träd, 5.   Unavoidable, Oundviklig, *ad.*

Trespass, Förbrytelse 3.   Unbecoming, Opassande.

Trial, Prof, 5. Ransakning, 2. Unburthen, Aflasta, *a.* 1.

Trick, Knep, 5. Konst, 3. Lek, 2. Unbutton, Upknäppa, *a.* 3.

Trifle, Lappri, 5. Småsak, 3. Uncertain, Oviss, *ad.*

Triple, Trefaldig, *ad.*   Uncivil, Ohöflig, *ad.*

Trot, Traf, *s. c.* Trafva, *a.* 1. Uncle, Farbror, or Morbror.

Trouble, Besvär, 5. Möda, 1. Undeniable, Oneklig, *ad.*

Trough, Träg, 5. Ho, 2.   Underbid, Missbjuda, *i.* 2.

True, Sann, Viss, Redlig, *ad.* Undermine, Undergräfva, 2.

Truth, Sanning, 2.   Underneath, Inunder.

Try, Försöka, *a.* 3. Sträfva, *a.* Understand, Förstå, *i.* 3.

Tub, Kar, 5. Balja, 1. [1. Understanding, Förstånd, *s. n.*

Tumour, Svullnad, 3.   Undertake, Företaga, *i.* 2.

Tune, Ton, 3. Ljud, 5.   Undertaker, Begrafvare, 5.

Turn, Vändning, 2. Fallenhet. Underwrite, Underskrifva.

Turn, Vända, *a.* 2. Svarfva, *a.* Underwriter, Assuradör, 3.

Turner, Svarfvare, 5.   [1. Undone, Förlorad, *ad.*

Turnip, Rofva, 1.   Undress, Afkläda, *a.* 2.

Swedish Turnip, Kålrot, 3. Undressed, Oklädd, *ad.*

Twilight, Skymning, *s. c.* Uneasy, Orolig, *ad.*

Twin, Tvilling, 2.   Unequal, Ölika, *ad.*

Twist, Tvinna, *a.* 1. Sno, *a.* 2. Uneven, Ojemn, *ad.*

Type, Förebild, 3. Styl, 2. Unexpected, Oförmodad, *ad.*

Unfair, Obillig, *ad.*

Ugly, Ful, Stygg, *ad.*   Unfit, Otjenlig, *ad.*

Ultimate, Slutlig, *ad.*   Unfold, Utveckla, *a.* 1.

Umbrella, Paraply, 3.   Unfortunate, Olycklig, *ad.*

Ungrateful, Otacksam, *ad.*

Uniform, Enformig, *ad.*

Union, Förening, 2.

Universal, Allmän, *ad.*

Unknown, Obekant, *ad.*

Unlawful, Olaglig, *ad.*

Unlimited, Oinskränkt, *ad.*

Unlucky, Olycklig, *ad.*

Unnecessary, Onödig, *ad.*

Unpaid, Obetald, *ad.*

Unpleasant, Obehaglig, *ad.*

Unprovided, Oförsedd, *ad.*

Unreasonable, Obillig, *ad.*

Unreserved, Öppenhjertig.

Unruly, Ostyrig, Tredsk, *ad.*

Unseen, Osedd, *ad.*

Unsettled, Ostadig, Yr, *ad.*

Unshaken, Fast, *ad.*

Unsteady, Ostadig, *ad.*

Unthought (of), Oförtänkt.

Untie, Knyta (up), *i.* 2. Lösa.

Untruth, Osanning, 2.

Unusual, Ovanlig, *ad.*

Unwieldy, Ovig, Tung, *ad.*

Upright, Rak, Uprigtig, *ad.*

Urge, Yrka, *a.* 1. Tränga, *a.* 2.

Urn, Urna, Kruka, 1.

Use, Bruk, 5. Bruka, *a.* 3.

Useful, Nyttig, Duglig, *ad.*

Usual, Vanlig, Bruklig, *ad.*

Usurer, Procentare, 5.

Usurp, Våldbruka, *a.* 1. 3.

Utter, Yttra, *a.* 1. Uttala, *a.* 1.

[3.

Vain, Fåfäng, Fruktlös, *ad.*

In vain, Förgäfves.

Valet, Betjent, 3.

Valley, Dal, 2. Däld, 3.

Value, Värde, 4. Värdera, *a.* 1.

Vanity, Fåfänga, *s. c.*

Vapour, Dunst, Vapör, 3.

Various, Mångfaldig, *ad.*

Vary, Förändra, *a.* 1.

Vault, Hvalf, Källare, 5.

Veal, Kalfkött, *s. n.*

Vegetables, Grönsaker, *p.*

Veil, Florshufva, 1. Dok, 5.

Vein, Ådra, 1.

Velvet, Sammet, 5.

Venal, Fal, *ad.*

Venetians blinds, Jalusier.

Venture, Våga, *a.* 1.

Verbal, Muntlig, *ad.*

Verdict, Utslag, 5. Dom, 2.

Verse, Vers, 3.

Very, Ganska.

Vessel, Fartyg, Kärl, 5.

Vex, Plåga, Reta, *a.* 1.

Vice, Last, 3. Odygd, 3.

Victim, Offer, 5.

Victory, Seger, 2.

Vie, Täfla, *a.* 1.

View, Syna, *a.* 1. Se, Bese, *i.* 3.
Vigour, Styrka, *s. c.* Kraft, 3.
Village, By, 2.
Vinegar, Ättika, *s. c.*
Violate, Oförrätta, *a.* 1.
Violence, Våld, 5. Häftighet.
Virtue, Dygd, 3.
Virtuous, Dygdig, *ad.*
Visible, Synlig, *ad.*
Voice, Röst, 3.
Vomit, Kräkas, *d.* 3.
Vow, Löfte, 4.
Voyage, Resa, (til sjös), 1.
Vulgar, Allmän, Gemen, *ad.*
Vulnerate, Såra, *a.* 1.

Wade, Vada, *a.* 1.
Wafer, Munlack, 5. Oblat, 3.
Waft, Vefta, *a.* 1. Öfverföra, *a.*
Wager, Vad, 5.
Wages, Lön, 3. Betalning, 2.
Waggon, Forvagn, 2.
Wainscot, Paneling, 2.
Waist, Medja, *s. c.* Veklif, 5,
Waistcoat, Vest, 2. Lifstycke.
Wait, Vänta, *a.* 1. Dröja, *a.* 2.
Wake, Vakna, *a.* 1.
Waken, Väcka, *a.* 3.
Walk, Spatsering, 2. Spatsera.
Wall, Vägg, Mur, 2.
Walnut, Valnöt, 3.

Wander, Vandra, *a.* 1.
Want, Behof, 5. Behöfva, *a.* 2.
War, Krig, 5.
Warble, Qvittra, Drilla, *a.* 1.
Warehouse, Magasin, 3.
Warm, Varm, *ad.* Värma, *a.* 2.
Warn, Varna, *a.* 1.
Warrant, Försäkra, *a.* 1.
Wasp, Geting, 2.
Waste, Slösa, *a.* 1. 3. Förspilla.
Watch, Vakt, 3. Ur, 5.
Watch, Vakta, Akta (på) *a.* 1.
Watchmaker, Urmakare, 5.
Watchman, Brandvakt, 3.
Water, Vatten, 5. Vattna, *a.* 1.
Waterman, Roddare, 5.
Wave, Väg, Våga, 1.
Waver, Vackla, *a.* 1.
Wax, Vax, *s. n.* Vaxa, *a.* 1.
Way, Väg, 2. Sätt, 5.
Weak, Vek, Svag, *ad.*
Weaken, Försvaga, *a.* 1.
Weakness, Svaghet, 3.
Wealth, Välmagt, Rikedom.
Wealthy, Rik, Förmögen, *a.*
Wear, Nöta, *a.* 3. Slita, *i.* 2.
Weary, Trött, *ad.* Trötta, *a.* 1.
Weather, Väder, 5. Väderlek.
Weave, Väfva, *a.* 2.
Wedding, Bröllop, 5.
Wedge, Kil, Vigge, 2.

Wedlock, Ägtenskap, 3.

Week, Vecka, 1.

Weep, Gråta, *a.* 2.

Weigh, Väga, *n.* 2.

Weight, Vigt, Tyngd, 3.

Well, Brunn, 2.

Wet, Våt, *ad.* Väta, *a.* 3.

Wheat, Hvete, *s. n.*

Wheel, Hjul, 5.

Wheel-barrow, Skott-kärra,

Whelp, Hvalp, 2. [1.

Wherefore, Hvarföre.

Whet, Bryne, 4. Bryna, *a.* 1.

Whey, Vassla, 1.

While, Stund, Tid, 3.

Mean While, Emedlertid.

Whim, Nyck, Vurm, 3.

Whip, Basa, Piska, *a.* 1.

Whipstaff, Rorkult, 2.

Whiskers, Mustacher, *p.*

Whisper, Hviskning, 2. Hviska.

Whistle, Pipa, 1. Pipa, *i.* 2.

White, Hvit, *ad.*

White-wash, Hvitlimma, a.

Whitsuntide, Pingst. [1.

Whole, Hel, *ad.*

Wholesale, Grosshandel, *s. c.*

Wholesome, Helsosam, *ad.*

Wick, Veke, 2.

Wicked, Elak, Ond, *ad.*

Wide, Vid, Stor, Bred, *ad.*

Widen, Vidga, Utvidga, *a. t.*

Widow, Enka, 1.

Widower, Enkling, 2.

Width, Vidd.

Wife, Hustru, 3.

Wig, Peruk, 3.

Wild, Vild, Rasande, *ad.*

Wilderness, Öcken, 2.

Wile, List, 3. Knep, 5.

Will, Vilja, *s. c.*

Willow, Pil, 2.

Wind, Vind, 2. Väder, 5.

Window, Fönster, 5.

Wine, Vin, 3. (p. 55).

Wink, Vink, 2. Vinka, *a.* 1.

Winter, Vintra, 2. Vintra *a* 1.

Wipe, Aftorka, *a.* 1.

Wire, Tråd, (messing, stål).

Wise, Vis, Förståndig, *ad.*

Wish, Önskan, *s. c.* Önska, *a.* 1.

Wit, Qvicket, 3. Förstånd, *s. n.*

Withdraw, Gå (*i.* 3.) bort.

Wither, Vissna, *a.* 1.

Witness, Vittne, 4. Vittna, *a.*

Wolf, Varg, Ulf, 2. [1.

Woman, Qvinna, 1.

Wonder, Under, 5. Undra, *a.*

Wonderful, Underlig, *ad.*

Wood, Skog, 2. Ved, *s. c.*

Wool, Ull, *s. c.*

Word,

Word, Ord, 5. Löfte, 4.

Work, Verk, 5. Arbete, 4.

Work, Arbeta, *a.* 1.

World, Verld, 2.

Worm, Mask, 2.

Worn, Nött, Brukad, *ad.*

Worship, Dyrkan, *s. c.* Dyrka.

Worsted-stockings, Ullstrum-

  por.

Worth, Värde, *s. n.* Förtjenst.

Wound, Sår, 5. Såra, *a.* 1.

Wreck, Skeppsbrott, Vrak, 5.

Wrap, Insvepa, *a.* 3.

Wreath, Krans, 2. Vrida, *a.* 3.

Wretch, Usling, 2. Stackare.

Wretched, Olycklig, Usel, *ad.*

Wright, Konstnär, 3.

Ship-Wright, Skeppsbyggare.

Wrinkle, Skrynka, 1.

Wrist, Vrist, Handled, 3.

Writ, Skrift, 3. Lagbref, 5.

Write, Skrifva, *i.* 3.

Writing-desk, Skrif-pulpet.

Wrong, Vrång, Orätt, *ad.*

I am wrong, Jag har orätt.

Wrong, Oförrätt, 3.

Wry, Sned, Vriden, *ad.*

Yard, Gård, Aln, 2. Rå, 3.

Yarn, Garn, *s. n.*

Yawn, Gäspa, *a.* 1.

Year, År, 5.

Yearly, Årlig, *ad.*

Yelk, Gula, 1.

Yellow, Gul, *ad.*

Yet, Dock, Ännu.

Yield. Medgifva, *i.* 2.

Yoke, Ok, 5.

Young, Ung, Späd, *ad.*

Youth, Ungdom, Yngling, 2.

Zeal, Nit, *s. n.* Ifver, *s. c.*

Zealot, Svärmare, 5.

Zodiac, Djurkrets, *s. c.*

Zone, Bälte, 4. Trakt, 3.

Zoology, Djurlära, *s. c.*

CPSIA information can be obtained at www.ICGtesting.com

230862LV00002B/280/P

9 781171 920182